An AWESOME .... *twork of homeschool families, has* ... *ion of homeschool realities. I was a homeschool mom for two years. Circumstances led us back into the norm. This book is just what I needed to realize that I am my children's best teacher and unschooling we will go again. Thank you! I recommend this book to everyone who has ever contemplated or criticized homeschooling.*

Leah Haldy-Fisher
Author of Echoes of The Heart
Owner of The Author Annex bookstore

If you're afraid of tackling homeschooling, you won't be when you finished this book. The practical advice and sweet rewards may just persuade you it's a challenge worth pursuing.

Terri Wagner
Editor

As a college educator, I found Steimle's collection a refreshing read. I have known many families who have homeschooled their children with tremendous success. Most of the homeschooled students I receive at the college level--some of them entering public school for the first time--are excellent students, eager to learn and grow. This book is a must read for anyone frustrated with traditional school paradigms at the secondary level and looking to homeschool.

Dr. Nicole Amare, Assistant Professor of English, the University of South Alabama.

Home Is Where The Learning Is:

Homeschool Lifestyles From Homeschool Moms

Written and Collected by
Valerie J. Steimle

10-Digit ISBN 1-59113-928-7
13-Digit ISBN 978-1-59113-928-7

The material included in this book has been written and compiled from the author's point of view. When it is decided to homeschool your children, please refer to and follow your state laws.

Printed in the United States of America.

Booklocker.com, Inc.
2006

Also by Valerie J. Steimle:

Home Is Where The Heart is

http://www.strengthenyourhome.com

This book is dedicated to all those parents
who take the time to educate their children.

Acknowledgments

This book has been a collective effort. I was the drive to get it started but I must thank all the homeschool mothers who came to my rescue with their writings. Lisa Odaffer, Debbie Hanson, Cherie Logan, Lisa Johnson, Karen Gibson, Gail Thomas and Donna Knox. Also all those mothers who contributed to the official publication for the Baldwin County Home Educators Association: Home's Cool Herald. All these mothers are dedicated educators and I am truly thankful for their contribution.

I also want to thank my family for putting up with me as I typed away at this book which took a year and a half to finish. There were also many homeschool parents who encouraged me to publish this book because they wanted to read it.

I also want to thank Angela Hoy for taking an interest in the book and publishing it for me.

Lastly but not least, I want to thank my Heavenly Father for giving me the inspiration for writing. I was always a poor reader but I have somehow overcome that and have been writing since I was twelve.

Table of Contents

Introduction

There are three aspects of life that are very dear to me: God, family and homeschool. This book is written about aspect number three: the lifestyle of learning at home. There are many opinions, controversies and discussions about homeschool and in these chapters; I want to educate those who do not understand what life is like for homeschooling families. If you have ever wondered about homeschool and what parents do for their children then this book would interest you. This book can also be helpful to those whom have already started homeschooling and would like to read about the different perspectives of what is done in families who homeschool and what their experience is

Ever since I was a little girl, I knew I would teach my own children. I didn't know at that time what "homeschool" was. I had read about Abraham Lincoln learning at home from reading books. I had learned in school about how some of our forefathers stayed home and learned. Somehow, my inklings as a young girl gave me the idea that I would like to teach my own children. I didn't think I was a better teacher than anybody else, but I felt, as a child, it was important to have them school at home. I just knew I would but I wasn't sure of when. I never knew anyone personally who was taught by their parents at home until I went to Ricks College in 1977. Onc of my professors had studied this type of learning and was writing a master's thesis on it. I believe it was at this time, in 1977, that some parents started homeschooling their children

This book has been written from eight perspectives with tips from several others. Some of the perspectives you will find here focus on how the family started homeschooling and others on the lifestyle they live. These experiences are from homeschool mothers whom I have known from friendship or whom I have met through my journey of homeschooling my own children. Some of these stories also tell of what mothers have done to overcome the learning disabilities in their children. They are phenomenal women with great words of wisdom.

Now for a reality check. Once you actually start homeschooling, you sometimes get to the point when you ask yourself, "Why am I doing this?" We have good days and we have bad days and many times a good encouraging word from other parents helps us to maintain our perspective. Reading about what other parents do in teaching their children is also helpful in learning new ways of teaching a concept for your own child because sometimes you can't think of a better way to get through. Or as one mother put it "I like touching base with people who are doing it successfully, get new ideas and to remind myself that I'm not insane".(See Chapter 3 for more Lisa Odaffer)

If you don't homeschool already, this book will give you a good idea of what goes on for homeschool families. If you do homeschool, then sit back and enjoy reading about other parents' successes. This is their story and I am your guide.

I am beginning to suspect all elaborate and special systems of education.
They seem to me to be built upon the supposition that every child is a kind of idiot who must be taught to think.
Whereas if the child is left to himself, he will think more and better, if less slowly.
Let him come and go freely, let him touch real things and combine his impressions for himself, instead of sitting indoors at a little round table while a sweet-voiced teacher suggest that he build a stone wall with his wooden blocks, or make a rainbow out of strips of colored paper, or plant straw trees in flower pots.
Such teaching fills the mind with artificial associations that must be got rid of before the child can develop independent ideas out of actual experiences.

--Ann Sullivan

Prologue: The Way Things Are...

By
Valerie J. Steimle

Before I go on to tell you about homeschooling, I want to explain the idea of "homeschool" itself.

Learning on earth for humans starts from the day they are born and ends when they die. Every person learns in their own way and in their own time. Parents who are interested in teaching their own children at home want the freedom to do so as they feel impressed to and other people don't always understand what that entails. Family and friends ridicule or make life difficult for these dedicated parents but the fact remains that these parents care enough about their children to keep them home and teach them what they need to know to make it on their own.

Originally the homeschool parents of the 70's wanted no government interference. They wanted the right to teach their children what they thought necessary to have an education. Thirty years later, state laws have been added and some school districts require the same subjects at home as there are in public school. The homeschooling movement is actually dividing itself into two groups. Homeschool families who use curriculum required by others whom they feel are the experts of teaching children and homeschool families who let their children learn from what they themselves find suitable for their own children. This might not be a traditional curriculum.

So for all practical purposes the term "homeschool" will refer to the method in which parents educate their children at home.

Along with this term comes a certain stigma which others seem to place in their minds when they hear about a family homeschooling their children. Either the parents are totally crazy to take on such a responsibility or are so ignorant their poor children won't learn anything in their life and will become total ignoramuses. You might ask yourself: "What about Benjamin Franklin, George Washington or Abraham Lincoln? They were all schooled at home and were great statesmen and United States leaders." But then you might think, "Well, that was a long time ago and there wasn't much to learn back then." From a speech given by John Taylor Gatto in 1991, a former public school teacher, "Pick up a fifth grade math or rhetoric textbook from 1850 and you'll see that the texts were pitched then on what would today be considered college level." (See www.johntaylorgatto.com)

As a society, we as parents are brainwashed into thinking we cannot teach our own children the academics. Mothers are convinced by the "experts" that they cannot give their own children the education necessary to make it in this world. This thinking is very twisted. Parents have always been responsible for teaching their children the correct principles of life and how to be courteous citizens and are very suited to teaching them the academics. In our modern world, we have become accustomed to sending our children off to school at the tender age of five to let someone else teach them.

Mothers have been teaching their children all along, just not as the public school dictates. Some parents might not realize this, but they are constantly teaching their children from the day they are born. Along with learning to tie their shoes and eating properly at the table, children watch their parents in whatever they do and learn. Those parents who read on their own, learn other tasks in their later life and follow their passions set a huge example for their children for the rest of their lives. Parents have the right to know by inspiration or research what they should teach their own children.

Homeschool parents go into the homeschool experience saying to themselves: "I am going to help my child learn what he/she needs to know to be educated. I have taken on the responsibility to teach my children and not depend on a stranger to teach them. I don't have to rationalize our lifestyle to others—I just do it".

So with all that in mind, you are now ready to read about the lifestyles of the homeschooled.

My schooling not only failed to teach me what it professed to be teaching,
But prevented me from being educated
To an extent which infuriates me when
I think of all I might have learned at home by myself.

--George Bernard Shaw

Chapter One
The Basics of Homeschool

By
Valerie J. Steimle

One of the first things I learned when I pulled my children out of public school and started teaching them at home was that parents are ultimately the people responsible for educating their children. As I mentioned earlier, they go along in life sending their children off to conventional school assuming their children would learn all they need to know and not worry about it again. It doesn't always work that way. I now have nine children and through them I have learned that they don't always catch on the same way. There are more ways to teach one concept to a child.

My children are as follows:

Sarah – now 21 and just married. She started off in public school in San Diego and then I pulled her out in 4th grade because of the over crowding in the school system due to a year-round school schedule the school district had switched to. We homeschooled for a year there until we moved to Alabama. She went back to public school because I wasn't prepared to homeschool in Alabama. Meaning, I didn't have the curriculum or know the state law at the time. The next year I started homeschooling her and from then on she never went back to public school. She is our poster child for home school. She graduated high school through a home school program, went on to graduate from a junior college and then graduated in May of 2003 from Auburn University in Animal Science. She has done very well in her schooling and I know without a doubt that homeschool works.

My next three, Naomi (19), Isaac (18) and Tasha (16) all were homeschooled sometime during the grade school experience but went to public school as well. All three started out in public school. I then pulled them out to homeschool at the same time as I did with Sarah. But by 9th grade they each decided they really wanted to go back to public school during their high school years. I (as well as they) felt that they could be motivated better by other teachers. High school work is very much independent study as a homeschool student and if you are not motivated to finish on your own it is very difficult to get through. A homeschooled high schooler really needs to be self-motivated. The other three also wanted to be on sports teams, which we could not always find in city leagues. I think Tasha spent the most time in public school out of any of them.

They all did very well during that time but there were drawbacks to returning to public school. Namely, the peer pressure of other students was there and having to keep the public school schedule whether you are burned out or not was also difficult. From the parent's perspective, there is the problem of not really knowing what is going on in the classroom. Sometimes I would find out about a problem one of them was having with a teacher almost after it was too late to help with the situation.

It was made apparent to me that public high school is just too stressful to enjoy (especially in the honor's program) and the time at home is so limited. I saw the personalities of all three become either withdrawn or mean. Then, by the 4th year, all three got "senioritis". That is to say, they didn't want to go to school anymore nor do their homework. It was difficult to watch this happening to my own children. They wanted to finish what they started and graduate but they didn't care anymore. A high school diploma can be obtained in three years. The fourth year seems to almost be a waste of time. Most of the classes they took that year were offered to them in college. If my children had homeschooled during that time they could have finished their high school diploma and been on to something else. Now there is the boredom that comes with having to sit through a class twice to get the credit. Once during high school and then again in college. My oldest who homeschooled all the way through took the more difficult high school courses at a junior college and only had to sit through it once.

Naomi is in her senior year at Huntingdon College in Montgomery, Alabama. She is planning to go on to graduate school in genetics. Isaac is a sophomore at the University of South Alabama in engineering and Tasha is a freshman at Brigham Young University. They all graduated in the top 15 of their high school class and do very well in college. Notice that they are all younger than the usual seniors, sophomores and freshman in college. I attribute that to the time they spent in homeschool. When they went back to public school they were simply too far ahead to go to what the school system considered their grade level and so they went ahead one year and did marvelously.

The next five are all being homeschooled through high school. We decided not to give these next five a choice. I think I am more able to handle the stress of the older homeschooled student and in the long run graduating through a homeschool high school curriculum is better.

Caleb (14) is already in his sophomore year in high school. Eliot (12) is doing a combination $7^{th}/8^{th}$ grade (as did the others); Lydia (9) is doing 3rd grade work and Moses (6) is in 1st grade. Henry (3) comes along for the ride.

Children have different learning styles and we as parents have to figure out what that learning style is. Children who are labeled "a trouble maker" or "learning disabled" could actually be quite intelligent but just learn from a different approach. For example, would your child rather *see* what they are supposed to do as opposed to handling it first or *listen* to an explanation? When you clump 15 to 20 students together it is difficult to get the individualized teaching that children sometimes need.

Do new sights distract the child? Do they remember things better if they see them first? If so, then the child is probably a visual learner. This is the most common way of learning.

Then, there is the auditory way, which is listening. I have one of those. Lydia (my nine-year-old) would much rather have all her school read to her then read it herself. For some reason she learns better that way.

Then, there is the kinesthetic or tactile learner. Or in other words, the feely, touchy child. This child has a hard time sitting still and is always grabbing for things. This child usually takes longer in the beginning to catch on. They are also the children "the experts" label "dyslexic". For some reason, I am most like the kinesthetic. I was never a good reader and I couldn't seem to sit still. I probably would have done better learning to read by feeling the letters rather than seeing the letters, but back in the sixties that was unheard of. I think the kinesthetic learner has a harder time learning because we as parents or teachers expect students to be visual learners. The need to touch in order to learn is much harder to teach.

Actually, your child can be all three but at times learning is easier if the teacher knows which learning approach is a better fit for your child. Especially for the kinesthetic.

So, if your child is having a difficult time learning in school you might consider some of these ideas with your child's teacher.

This reminds me of a story about a boy who was described by others as "retarded, addled, troublesome, precocious and mischievous". But "Little Al", as he was called, was the seventh child to Nancy Elliot who was a devout Presbyterian, and she never gave up on him. He was always very curious about things, which usually led to some kind of trouble. (Like burning down his father's barn) His mother learned that he was a hands on learner and was bored by the classroom routine, doodling and daydreaming to wile away the hours. After Al overheard a conversation with some teachers about how "addled" he was and that school for him would be a waste of time, his mother pulled him from public school and nurtured his education with books. She "implanted in his mind the love of learning" and he became a "voracious" reader. She kept him on the right path of learning which was a blessing for the rest of the world because Thomas Alva Edison, as he is better known, found solutions to problems towards the end of the 1800's which would usher in the new age of technology. He had many inventions including an improved stock ticker machine, kinescope, motion picture camera, phonograph and my personal favorite: the light bulb. Mr. Edison was heard to say: "My mother was the making of me. She understood me; she let me follow my bent. She cast over me an influence which has lasted all my life. [1]"Wouldn't that be great if we could all do for our children what Nancy Elliot Edison did for hers?

Mrs. Edison shows us one viewpoint common to most all homeschool families: that her child was not stupid and that she could do a better job meeting his unique educational needs.

Homeschool families also usually desire a simpler, self-reliant lifestyle and they are concerned with restoring traditional family roles and strengthening the church that they attend. They really care about the world around them and for the most part involve themselves in some grass roots organization to help this cause along. [2]

From Dr. Raymond and Dorothy Moores' *The Successful Homeschool Family Handbook,* comes this list of eight common characteristics of homeschoolers.

This is from a consensus of studies in 1994:

1) Home-educated children are highly competent socially, seldom age-segregated, and generally respectful of their parents.

2) The children study a full range of conventional and enrichment subject matters.

3) The average annual family income is around $25,000. (This might be surprising)

4) Most parents have some college education.

5) Most have definite philosophical or religious convictions and high moral values, although homeschool rationales reach far beyond religious views to include family integrity, desire for children to excel, and examples of successful neighbors and friends.

6) There are nearly three children per family.

7) Curricula vary widely from extremely flexible programs to quite formal teaching.

8) Children are taught with a great deal of warm parental responsiveness and camaraderie in study, work and service. They develop an adult level of reasonability five to eight years sooner than conventionally schooled students. [3]

If you know any homeschool family personally, they would probably fit into any number of those characteristics, which are not only an asset to their community but also a benefit to the children themselves.

Just as there are different learning styles of our children there are also different educational styles. I think it would be beneficial to list them here so you can understand the basic approaches of homeschooling.

Common Educational Approaches

Textbook Approach

Traditional: In the traditional approach, parents use graded textbooks and/or workbooks. They follow a certain schedule for the entire school year of 180 days. There are usually teacher's manuals, tests and record keeping materials that correspond to each text and workbook. This material is also available on the computer. You can also find these kinds of courses or "curriculum" through some public school districts, through private schools, through companies that sell pre-packaged curriculums or parents can pick and choose by buying directly from textbook publishers.

Non-Textbook Approach

Classical: Children under age 18 are taught the tools of learning known as "The Trivium". The Trivium has three parts. Each part corresponds to a childhood developmental stage.

Stage 1: Grammar Stage: Early elementary ages focuses on reading, writing, and spelling, study of Latin, developing observation, listening and memorization skills. The goal of this stage is to develop a general framework of knowledge and to acquire basic language arts and math skills.

Stage 2: Dialectic Stage: This stage starts about the age of middle school. Children begin to demonstrate independent or abstract thought, which is molded and shaped by teaching logic discussion, debate and how to draw correct conclusions and support them with facts.

Stage 3: Rhetoric Stage: This is the final phase of the Trivium which seeks to produce a student (usually by 15 years of age) who can use language, both written and spoken eloquently and persuasively.

Unit Study Approach: A Unit Study takes a theme or topic (a unit of study) and investigates deeply into all there is to know about that topic, integrating language arts, science, social studies, math and fine arts. Instead of studying seven or eight separate, unrelated subjects, all the subjects are blended together. For example, a unit study on bears could include reading and writing about bears (language arts). You could also include famous biologists who studied bears, studying their body parts, eating habits and life cycles (science). You could calculate the body fat needed to hibernate all winter (math) and learn about the habitats and ecological impact on their life. You could learn to sketch bears and so on until you have learned everything there is to know about bears.

The Living Books Approach: This approach is based on the writings of Charlotte Mason, a turn-of-the-century British educator. She felt that educating a child was preparing them for life and helping that child to live the fullest right now. She believed in respecting children as persons, involving them in real-life situations and allowing them to read really good books instead of what she called "twaddle"- worthless, inferior teaching material. This approach is probably best for elementary aged children. They are taught good habits, to be involved in a broad spectrum of real-life situations, and given ample time to play, reflect and create. Young children were not to have formal lessons at all. But when children are at an older age she would use what she called "living books" to educate. For example, for literature the children would read the classics. For history, she would pick historical biographies. For geography: well-written travel books. In art, the children would study great art pieces. If the children couldn't read they would be read to. Arithmetic is not mentioned at all but I suppose you could add this in for a well-rounded education.

The Principle Approach: This approach uses three American Christian concepts: the knowledge of our Christian history, an understanding of our role in the spread of Christianity and the ability to live according to the Biblical principles upon which our country is founded. Learning is based on seven principles: 1) Individuality, 2) self-government, 3) Christian Character, 4) A person's conscience is the most sacred of property, 5) The Christian Form of Government, 6) How the seed of local self-government is planted and 7) The Christian principle of American Political Union.

The belief here is that God has given us principles that govern every area of life: politics, education, and business. These areas of focus make up the curriculum for this approach. This kind of learning has been misunderstood as a history course but it is not. It does involve the study of much American history and encourages the use of notebooks for recording information. The whole emphasis as Mary Pride tells us is "on reasoning through basic principles rather than regurgitating facts." Thus the principle approach.

The Unschooling Approach: This is probably the hardest approach to explain and least understood. Unschooling is letting the children learn through their own desires and curiosities. It is the least structured learning approach. This allows children to pursue their own interests with parental support and guidance. The child is surrounded by a rich environment of books, learning resources and adults who model a lifestyle of learning. John Holt had started this style of homeschool. His motto was "trust children". He believed that children really want to learn and that they will learn what they need to know if left entirely to themselves. This style of learning is particularly scary for parents. There is always that doubt in the back of the mind, "Is my child learning all that he/she needs to learn to be an educated person?" I have known several families to use this method and they like it.

The Mixed Approach (also known as Eclectic): Many homeschoolers use a blend of the different approaches. I think that is the best way to educate and I have used this approach throughout most of my homeschool experience. Parents can use the best ideas from all the different approaches. I think strictly using one approach can limit what a child will learn. For example, you can use traditional math and science textbooks, but use unit studies around historical periods and geography. Then maybe use a computer program to teach typing and foreign language. I really like the idea of learning history through historical biographies. I have used this approach many times.

There is a lot to think about when trying to decide whether you want to homeschool your children. It seems scary at first, but with good preparation and lots of praying, it can be done at any time in your children's life. Some women (as you will read) know they want to homeschool from the time they give birth to their first child. Other women don't really know they want to homeschool until their child is already in 3rd grade. At times, public school will accentuate learning problems and it becomes obvious to the parent that something more needs to be done. I have known some mothers who pulled their children out of middle school, homeschooled for a year or two, and then let them go back for high school. There are many different ways to educate your child and at any age.

As you begin to think about whether you want to homeschool your children keep in the back of your mind several important points. This will be helpful to find out before you pull your child out of traditional school and start your actual learning time.

1) What does my state law say about homeschooling?

2) What kind of curriculum will I use?

State Laws

Every state in the United States of America says something in their law books pertaining to homeschooling. According to the Homeschool Legal Defense Association, there are four areas which states are divided into for homeschool requirements.[4]

1. States requiring no notice: The state does not require parents to initiate any contact with the school district when they decide to homeschool their children.

States: Alaska, Idaho, Indiana, Illinois, New Jersey, Michigan, Missouri, Oklahoma, and Texas.

2. States with low regulation: The state requires parents to notify their school district of their intention of homeschooling.

States: Alabama, Arizona, California, Delaware, Kansas, Kentucky, Montana, Mississippi, New Mexico, Nebraska, Nevada, Wisconsin, Wyoming, and Washington DC.

Homeschooling in my home state of Alabama, as in many other states, also requires you to be registered with a school of some kind or be a certified teacher. This school is called a "Legal Umbrella". It could be a private school or church school but this law requires the administrator to collect attendance records, which shows proof of participation.

3. States with moderate regulation: Parents are to send notification, test scores, and or professional evaluation of student progress.

States: Arkansas, Colorado, Connecticut, Florida, Georgia, Hawaii, Iowa, Louisiana, Maryland, New Hampshire, North Carolina, Ohio, Oregon, South Carolina, South Dakota, Tennessee, and Virginia.

With this requirement, many homeschool umbrellas will set up testing for their students and assign a certified teacher to meet quarterly with the parents. Some schools use a "portfolio" as part of the student progress report, which is just a sampling of the student's work through out the year.

4. States with high regulation: State requires parents to send notification or achievement test scores and or professional evaluation, plus other requirements. (i.e. curriculum approval by the state, teacher qualification of parents, etc.)

States: Maine, Massachusetts, Minnesota, New York, North Dakota, Pennsylvania, Rhode Island, Utah, Vermont, Washington and West Virginia.

This is pretty severe and there is less freedom for the parent to teach what they wanted. Curriculum is assigned from the grade level and you must follow a certain schedule of work. This is basically public school at home. The federal mandate for all public schools is to have 180 days attendance and as a requirement, each family would be required to fulfill that mandate.

Some parents feel that their rights are being taken away by the state. They want to make the decision about what is right for their child and not be forced to follow what some state bureaucrat has decided was good for every child in that state. There are intense debates; big lectures and long articles written on this very subject. All of this discussion can promote freethinking and might even help change state laws to be better than they are, but, for the time being it's best to follow your own state law. You might ask why this has to be. There have been numerous conflicts between school districts and families that homeschool. If you are abiding by the law of your state you have no cause to worry whether the state will investigate why you are homeschooling. If you aren't following the laws, then there are drastic measures that the state can take, including taking away your own children.

Curriculum

As for the curriculum you use there are many to choose from and much to read about. Right now there are thousands of web sites, workshops, book fairs and companies of curriculum, which specialize in this homeschool arena. Many times curriculum can be very overwhelming to a new homeschool parent.

When parents ask me what kind of curriculum they should use for their children, I tell them they need to find out for themselves what their own children need to learn. Homeschool for parents then takes on an everlasting job of finding out exactly what their children need to learn in their life until they get out on their own. This is sometimes done by trial or error but there are some points you can keep in mind.

1. There is a great deal of study involved before you start.

One thing I have learned after attending numerous homeschool curriculum fairs is that you need to study up on the different types of catalogues, lesson manuals, books, computer programs and other materials before going to those fairs. You can find much of this on the Internet by typing "homeschool" into a search engine. You can also ask other homeschool families what they use. If you don't know any, find out about your local association meetings and ask questions. Or you can read about curriculums from companies willing to send you a free catalogue. Then, when you go to a curriculum fair for the first time, DO NOT BUY ANYTHING. Just look at what is there. Then, leave. The next day go back and look again. If you still feel strongly about buying something (especially the $200-$300 sets) then make an educated purchase. I have heard from many parents that the biggest mistake they make is that they spend big money on a curriculum they don't know much about and then end up not wanting to use it and then they are stuck. All that can be avoided if you do some research on what is available.

2. If you do make the mistake of buying the wrong kind of curriculum, don't make the mistake of pushing your children into finishing the whole book. Either pick bits and pieces out to use through out the year or just resell it to someone else and start over.

But don't despair about the curriculum. Start early enough before you have to actually home school so you will have time to decide. For example: if you have a preschooler at the age of 3 or 4, that would be a good time to start looking around and studying what options you have to teach your child. You don't always have to start a child at the age of five.

If there is an emergency where you have to pull your child out of school right away, contact your local homeschool association. Many times you can find second hand books suitable in an emergency and they will know the state law requirements. This does happen quite often. But with genuine concern for your child and persistent parental study, you can get through anything.

Homeschool is such a challenging opportunity. I say challenging because it can test your patience with your own children and make you feel as if you didn't learn anything when you went to school. I say opportunity because your child will have the chance to learn at home in a comfortable environment. Who ever said having the same age group peers help children to learn appropriate behavior? Being in the company of adults regulates how a child should act. Remember "The Lord of the Flies"? At home, there are no drugs, no high stress demands from teachers, no peer pressures, no sassy mouths to contend with. I think teenagers would not talk back to their parents so much if they were respectful to what their parents were doing for them. Also there is no audience from other teenagers outside your family. In homeschooling, you also get to decide what your children will learn. There are no state mandates and no school authorities breathing down your neck.

You also have to remember that public school is a modern invention. It has been only in the last 150 years of human history that we have had this public school system to teach our own children. Parents used to educate their children or find a tutor to do it for them in their own home. So this system is still really being tested and the trouble spots are still being resolved.

Another added bonus for homeschooling is that you will learn all that you missed from school and at the end of the day; you feel that you really accomplished something. It is much more satisfying than a regular 9 to 5 job. Best of all, you will learn to love your child like no one else ever has. You will get closer to each other, which builds a great parent-child relationship.

I know I have come to appreciate the process of teaching my children what they need to know. I have seen the benefits of homeschool in many families as well as my own. We are closer together, we talk more and I can solve conflicts my children have before they get out of hand. If I had to do it over again, I would still homeschool all of my children. My efforts were well worth the time that I spent with them. They are intelligent, caring and hard working people and for the most part have learned what they needed to know to have a good well-rounded education. I hope this book will help you find what is best for your family and will help you make an educated decision of whether you would like to homeschool your own children.   Happy Homeschooling.

It is, in fact, nothing short of a miracle

that the modern methods of instruction have not yet entirely

strangled the holy curiosity of inquiry,

for this delicate little plant, aside form stimulation

stands mainly in need of freedom.

--Albert Einstein

Chapter Two
Living the Homeschool Lifestyle Over a Lifetime

by Cherie Logan
A Home Schooling Mother since 1985
www.noblechild.com

When I was pregnant with my 9th baby, Neil and I went to our favorite restaurant in San Diego. It was so crowded that the line went out the door and down the sidewalk. We found ourselves in line behind another very pregnant woman. As the line slowly moved forward, we struck up a conversation. I asked her if her baby would be her first. She replied that it was her second. She continued to talk about her pregnancy for a few minutes and then asked if my baby was my first. Neil said nothing, knowing what was about to happen.

"No, this is my ninth."

"Nine! You're kidding!" I just smile. Then she said, "You must have easy labors."

I nod my head and agree. "Yes, my fifth baby was only five contractions." I continued past her envious stare by saying, "But I have to go to bed or sit on the couch for nearly the entire pregnancy to get to that easy labor, and then I have had most of them at home."

She's stunned, wondering how anybody could do that. Neil is trying to not smile. Finally, she thinks she has it all figured out and says, "I bet you love it when school starts!"

With a wicked gleam in my eye, I move in for the final shock, "Yes, I look forward to school every year. I have always home schooled them and I enjoy returning to our normal routine." The poor lady could barely pick herself up off the floor in time to move to her table. Neil was chuckling and leaned over to whisper, "You love that, don't you?" And I do! I really love the shocked expressions and the clear message that we do things quite differently. However, I didn't mention to her that things do not always go smoothly. Like this day I recorded in my 1996 journal:

I didn't get out of bed until quite late. Neil had been up with the baby since about 7:30. He was sitting on the floor with her and watching the weather channel. I had asked that he get the children up, clothed, fed and morning jobs done so I could start school at 9 am. I was already way off schedule.

When I came in and asked if these things were done he said, "I have been trying to watch the weather channel." Then I saw my dear children.

I asked Chiya (rather skeptically), "Are you dressed?" She said, "Half-way." Good. Math has just been covered.

Ben said, "I have to shower." Wonderful. Health lesson has been done.

Nathan wanted to know what to have for breakfast. "Whatever you can find." I grumbled. Great! Home Economics and Self Sufficiency in one fell swoop!

Ryan and Cheyanne were already scavenging in the kitchen taking a bite or two out of apples and a taste of this and that. Hey...I'm on a role with an interactive history lesson: How early Hunters and Gatherers lived.

Chani and Chamrie were safely elsewhere. Chalk one up for Government and Delegation Class as they are the ones who fill in when Dad is watching the weather channel. I think we are failing this class.

We then had Family Scripture study and our Articles of Faith lesson. Then I read the first chapter of Swiss Family Robinson to the eager listeners amid the cries of little Chalae, the chatter of Ryan and Cheyanne and the workings of the washing machine and dryer.

To top it off, Neil was in the room trying winter coats on each of the children.
Shortly afterwards, I was informed that lunch time had arrived AND it was 1:00 PM so school should be over!

My journal entry ends with this determined declaration: "Tomorrow, we start at NINE AM SHARP!"

My 19th September of home schooling my children is rapidly approaching and thank goodness most days are not like the one I just shared with you! I am not the same woman today as I was when I had my first little kindergartner. I had sent over 50 letters to various companies and organizations trying to find a curriculum that would be perfect for our family. Of course, I had no idea what perfect really was....every thought concerning home schooling was new and walked the edge of counter-culture.

Neil and I married in June 1978. Two weeks later I was elated to discover that I was pregnant. In 22 years of living, I had never experienced anything like this! The fairy-tale existence of a new bride combined with the overwhelming emotional roller coaster of pregnancy was all-encompassing. Neil never knew what to expect from me.

One moment I was organizing my castle and the next I was sobbing in the kitchen, unable to decide which dish to wash first. And I cried. For three months I cried every day. Not all day of course, just every time Neil had to walk out the door and leave me alone.
The day came when Neil entered our bedroom and found me sitting on the bed, watching my belly move. I tried to get him to feel our baby, but every time his hand touched the kicking spot, our little one quieted down. I was enthralled. Nothing...nothing could ever be like this! The awful part of pregnancy was gone and replaced by the miracle. I was going to be a mother!

Life changed suddenly in January. I became a mother much sooner than expected. Our little son was born 6 weeks premature and weighed 3 pounds 6 ounces. He struggled to breathe and was taken to Children's Hospital in San Diego. That first night of motherhood found me in one hospital, my son in another and my husband asleep at home. Now I cried for real. My heart was breaking. All I wanted in the entire world was to hold my baby and be held by my husband.

The next 8 ½ weeks moved at an exhaustingly slow pace. Every day found us at the hospital, watching, touching, and talking to our little angel. We noticed that when we were with our tiny son his vital signs would improve. Marshall was on a drug that paralyzed his little body so he wouldn't fight the machine breathing for him. He shouldn't have had any control over his body and yet every time we whispered to him that we had to leave, he would struggle to open his eyes. Our hearts told us that he was trying to get us to stay, just a little longer.

Suddenly, too quickly, the day came when I held my son while my husband held me. I cuddled my little Marshall and the world faded away. There was no existence anywhere outside of our little circle of love. Then my sweet Neil, his heart breaking, whispered, "He's gone. Our son is gone."

The weeks and months that followed were filled with intense and sometimes vague emotions. Motherhood had eluded me. Never had I ever envisioned this! Where did I fit in? I wasn't like the women who were raising children....I had never brought my baby home. I wasn't like the women whose children had grown and left home.. those women had years of raising their babies. I wasn't like the women who couldn't have children. I could...I did...and I was alone.

Then something settled deep in my heart. A great comfort and understanding washed over me as I realized that I was indeed a mother.

That I was a mother who had experienced a lifetime with her baby. A lifetime...no matter its length...a lifetime of love, experience, and perspective. A sweet lifetime...my son's entire life.

When my beautiful, full-term Chani was placed in my arms, the wonder of life permeated everything I did. And the commitment to be her mother for a lifetime filled my soul. I held her, cuddled her, comforted her, and taught her. I marveled at her accomplishments and was delighted with her giggles. I was amused by her play and comforted by her kisses. I grew so much just being Chani's mother that I was relieved when her bedtime arrived so that I could renew myself for the next day's adventures.

When this little angel was 11 months old, I read an article about home schooling. I had never suspected that there were alternatives to public school. Instantly and deeply I knew that in order to have Chani stay the delightful person that she was, I needed to teach her at home. I knew the same would be true of all my children. It was an inner commandment, not just an idea or suggestion...but the powerful and undeniable voice of the spirit. Well...I had time to explore this new concept…after all...Chani was just turning 1 year!

But time has a way of inching along and rushing by. It seemed that suddenly my oldest was 5, my next was 3, my youngest was a year-and-a-half, we had another baby due in a few months...and our great home school experiment was upon us.

Now . . . the practical stuff started crowding in on me, the curriculums, the organization, the scheduling, the worry, the inspiration . . . there were so many parts to being a home schooling mom. If I was going to survive home schooling an ever growing family, I'd have to discover what worked best for us.

I want to share with you the concepts that have worked for our family. As I do, I hope that you will find yourselves adapting them to your particular life. It doesn't matter whether you homeschool for twenty years or only for one, you will want to enjoy the process and be able to make guilt-free decisions when faced with frustrating situations. These concepts will help you do that once you have adjusted them to suit your unique family.

The five elements that I believe go into our family's home schooling are:

1. Developing the Long View – the Purpose.
2. Philosophies which guide behavior to match view.
3. Structure to support the view.
4. Communication skills to enrich understanding and bring us to eternal companionship with our children
5. Attitude Management because it is the attitude that keeps the fire lit.

First – Purpose

My specific purpose is that we are raising our children to be independent learners, successful husbands and wives, loving and capable mothers and fathers, good friends, and service oriented, moral adults.

When I first started home schooling the most frequently asked questions were: How long will you do this . . . forever? What about High School? Are you going to teach algebra? I would smile and answer: I don't know about forever, but I'm doing it this year. Chani is only 5; she has a few years before High School. And to the last question I would say, "Oh, my children are not allowed to learn algebra until they leave home!"

As long as homeschooling fulfills the reason we are doing it, we will continue. We are home schooling our children first because the Lord promised us that if we wanted our children to keep the spirit he sent with them, that we would home school.

Secondly, we are convinced that it is the very best lifestyle for our family and will allow each child to develop their unique personalities and prepare them for the important responsibilities and relationships of adulthood.

Discovering what I wanted for my children wasn't an overnight awakening. At first, I didn't want to think about my little ones as adults. I wanted to be careful to not put any limits or expectations upon them. There is a belief that parents who do that push their children or hold them back. It took a while for me to realize there were differences between saying you want your child to be a doctor or a lawyer and saying that you want your child to be a successful husband or wife.

Step by step I discovered what I wanted for my children. With each step, I became more confident in evaluating the things that will help me prepare them for those important roles. With a solid purpose behind our home schooling adventure, days like the one from my journal become like a summer shower interrupting a game. We rest a bit and wait for the rains to blow past.

Second: Philosophy Guides Our Behavior to Match Our Purpose.

There are several philosophical concepts I believe will best bring about the purpose we have established for our family. I'm going to touch on five of them.

A. One of our philosophies is that our actions need to be based on our long term goal and not on what seems to be immediately preferable.

I can clean up after dinner and wash dishes much faster than any of my children, regardless of their age. This is a law of nature – parents get the job done better, faster, and with less whining than children! However, if my goal is to not have some future son or daughter-in-law grumble at me and if I want my children be successful husbands and wives, then I would be wise to assign the task to my children, even if it takes an hour longer to finish.

As a teaching mom, I know that my preschoolers enjoy watching wonderful educational programs. This entertainment can occupy them quietly for several minutes. However, I also know that my older children… again, regardless of their age…will stop whatever they are doing to watch the same shows.

Because I am focused on the long term purpose of my children becoming independent learners, I find I have to arrange their learning environment by scheduling when educational programs can be viewed. This doesn't mean that the younger ones won't ask every day if they could watch something and it certainly doesn't mean that they will never fuss at me when I say no. The short term effect of my scheduling is a real trial in daily patience, but the future benefits strengthen my resolve.

There are times when the long-term vision gets crowded out by necessity. Rainy days happen. Over-scheduling and illnesses intrude on the normal daily flow. Taking a day off to watch six hours of *Pride and Prejudice* or surviving through a day long game of monopoly makes for a pleasant mental and emotional vacation. These occasional days do wonders for creating new energy when you begin to refocus. Be flexible and accept these diversions as part of the living process. These vacations are normal and ultimately desirable because they renew everybody's energy. Because there is an established long-term purpose, these little vacations will not crash your entire program.

B. The second philosophical concept centers around teaching and learning. How you view these two processes will determine how you manage your curriculum.

Over the years we have developed a teaching and learning philosophy that works well for us. Basically, it goes like this:

Teaching is the parent's job. Learning is the child's job. What, when and where teaching is done is the parent's responsibility. How teaching is done is based upon the child's personality, the family interaction and the parent's comfort level. This doesn't mean that the parent never learns and the child never teaches, but when it comes to responsibility, parents teach, children learn.

We feel it is our responsibility to determine if our child will be taught at home, at private or public school or a combination of places. It is also our responsibility to decide on a curriculum for our children. We have the task of forming a schedule that is compatible with our family's needs. Our job includes evaluating each child's strengths and weaknesses and plan a course of private study to compliment the group lessons. Once these things are worked out and teaching begins, then it is our child's responsibility to learn. Learning means following the instructions, the outlines, and the schedules presented. Learning consists of listening, thinking, creating and remembering.

When something interferes with this learning process than it is my job to find out where the problem lies. Will a change in teaching technique overcome the difficulty? What about a change of schedule? What about more repetition? More physical or creative work? If something doesn't work then I try something else until everything begins to run smoothly.

Sometimes, the learning problem is centered in my child. He could be having a rebellious day, she could be lazy and whiney about doing the work. At this point, I need to recognize that the responsibility for the behavior belongs to my child. He is the one who has the job of learning. If I have provided all the tools and made adjustments to suit his learning style and he still refuses, then it is time to work on attitudes. The first attitude assessment needs to be my own. Am I being stubborn when a little negotiation will work wonders? Have I taught clearly? How important is the thing being resisted in relation to our Purpose? After my own evaluation, I need to evaluate my child. Is he getting enough sleep? Is he skipping breakfast to play on the computer? Is it stubbornness or laziness?

Once the assessments are made, then it is time to take action to overcome the problem. There are a few courses of action that we consistently use. The first is that there will be no playing with friends until school work is finished. The other is that school continues until a specific hour and then is done. This may seem to be in conflict but having the two different norms in our home allows me to decide which one is best under various situations, and because they are both used frequently, my children consider it consistent.

When it comes to teaching, a parent's comfort level comes into play concerning subject matter. If I am not comfortable teaching something, then my children can choose to learn more themselves, my husband can teach it, I can find a tutor for that topic, send the child to school for the one class, get a home study college class with a mentor following the child's progress, or even decide that learning a particular subject can wait until the child is grown and learning on his own.

C. The third philosophy we follow concerns priorities:

We all have priorities in life. Sometimes they are obscured by the busy nature of our daily activities. By spending some time focusing on priorities we can make choices which are in keeping with our home schooling goals.

Through establishing priorities we develop our own yardstick to measure the use and abuse of our time. We are better able to make intelligent and guilt-free decisions in a wide variety of situations.

Make a priority list pertaining to homeschooling – what you want your children to study, what is important for the day to go right, etc. Your list will be quite long and you know there is no way you can cover everything every day. Then go through the prioritizing process. Check the first item against the next. As long as the first is the most important, continue checking it. If one item becomes more important than the first, then pick up that one and check it against the remaining. (At that point you have your top two priorities. Continue until you have a list of the top ten priorities.)

If the first five things on your priority list are covered you can consider that you have had a successful day. However, if you are finding that you are worried about how school is going or about how you are doing with organizing the day, then it is time to look at your list. You will probably find that the first five things are not being consistently accomplished. Use this list to keep yourself on track.

On stressed days, do the top three things. On more productive days, do as many as you can. It is the over-all view that matters here. If you are hitting the top three, four or five items consistently, you will feel successful in your school.

There is a draw-back to this. Very few children have the same priorities as their parents. There are not many who would put school work before playing with friends. As their mother, I have a longer view of what is important. It is my job to enforce my priority of school work over theirs of no schoolwork – or choose that today, play is more important! It would be nice if they always loved what they had to do but some things in life are done just because they must be, regardless of how we feel about them.

D. Our fourth next philosophy concept is: There is time, eventually, to learn whatever is important to learn.

Everything doesn't have to all be learned today or even this year. Keeping a long view and staying centered in the reason you are living a homeschool lifestyle helps you relax through the frustrations. Give yourself time to learn the techniques that work best in your home. Give your child time to blossom. The future is made up of all the small components called Right Now...relax and enjoy those moments.

E. Our fifth home schooling philosophy is: I don't have to do everything, teach everything, understand everything.

In fact, if I had to do, teach and understand everything, then eventually the important things in life would fall apart because I'd be striving for an impossible goal! When I am not comfortable with a subject, I find a tool or another person to teach it. Grandparents can be great mentors. My mother has pointed out a few areas that need my children's attention. It was wonderful to have her help in the area of social etiquette! There are computers, videos; friends to tutor, classes, and always remember that children will grow up...some things can wait until they are adults.

Remember that just because you can do something doesn't mean that you should. If you are doing all the teaching, cleaning, cooking, shopping, and organizing, will you have time to read to your toddler, nurse your baby, work on your hobby, have dates and planning sessions with your husband, relax and watch television, exercise, or sleep? If you are the one doing everything will your child be prepared to be a mother or father, a wife or husband, to live on their own, or to have experience working with and teaching another person?

Simplify your life through scheduling meals, shopping, and chores. See your working self as a supervisor and organizer rather than as the cook and cleaning lady. When your children are tiny you have to do almost everything that needs doing in the home. As they grow those jobs should shift more and more away from you and towards the children as they learn how to care for their needs and those of others. By the time they leave your home, your children should be able to cook, clean, teach, help others and organize their lives. I suggest a visit to Flylady.com for a proven and easy method for getting control of home schedules.

The Third Aspect of Living this Lifestyle is to Develop the Structure to Support Your Purpose of Home Schooling.

Structure is the form and function of your goal. What curriculums will you use? What routines will you follow? What schedules work for your family? After developing your purpose and philosophy, then you need to create a structure for your school day. Expect the structure to change from time to time as you experiment with new ideas.

In our home we use three methods that work well together. The first is my own style, developed over almost 20 years of homeschooling. It consists of group lessons and private studies. The group lesson ideas can be found in my book *The Noble Child Experience.* We use Dr. Glenn Kimber's guide books. They allow me freedom by not telling me what I should do every day yet giving me a solid base to present to my children. The last method we consistently use comes from Dr. Oliver DeMille. It is composed of reading, discussing, and developing family classics for group study and personal reading. I show some examples of how to use this method in getting more meaning out of the books you read and the movies you watch in my book, Becoming a Mother of Noble Children.

By the time my older girls became teens they were pretty independent in pursuing their interests. They join us for group lessons and I made suggestions for their continued learning. It has been a joy to watch them develop talents and pursue worthy interests. One son is following this same pattern, but my other two sons do best when I clearly outline what was expected for them in educational matters. It takes a different type of work on my part to encourage them to enter the self-learning stage than it did to keep track of the others self-directed interests.

I have found that my family needs a combination of group lessons and private studies. The private studies allow each child to work on what they need at their unique level. Group lessons provide unity among my children and make teaching much easier for me.

I like to pair up my children during some lessons by putting an advanced reader work with a less skilled reader. This encourages the children to help and learn from each other. I evaluate my children's private studies and my group lessons frequently, giving the younger children a check-off list of what they need to do and discussing study goals with my youth.

We do our morning jobs before school starts, most evening jobs just before dinner and a few right after. During school time, I don't worry about the chaos that teaching nine children makes in a home.

Once the school hours have ended, I find that it is a good idea to have the children play for awhile rather than to immediately attack their afternoon chores. This gives me a little breather before supervising the clean up and helps the children stay focused on school knowing that once it is over, they can get together with their friends for the afternoon. They need to do the chores before dinner. I will often set a time for pre-dinner chores that is an hour or so before our meal. If they finish those chores early, they can continue playing with their friends. This helps them to hurry with the chores, and even *decide on their own* to do them before play rather than be interrupted in the middle of it!.

Structure management takes creativity and assessment. While the home schooling purpose will change a little over the years and philosophies will slowly refine over time, the home and school structure should be allowed to adapt according to Mother's discretion.

The Fourth Important Element is Family Communication

I believe that family communication is vital in home schooling. Of all the skills I have to use as a mother and teacher, this is the one that gets used constantly. I've developed a 32 hour course on family communication called Becoming Crystal Clear. I can't even begin to share with you all of the information I feel is important in strengthening the family through the study of personal, family and social language. But I do hope to spark an interest in you that will lead to a study of this subject.

For today's talk, I've narrowed my focus to one small part of communicating with the youth. If you have youth already, you'll be nodding your head as I mention these stages. If your children are young, it will give you some ideas to ponder over the next few years. I frequently remind myself, my husband and my children that I am raising my peers in the eternities. My children are children for such a short time, and if I want to keep a closeness to them that extends beyond those years, I need to keep a view of what I want out of our adult relationship.

The responsibility of adapting to my children's maturing status rests with my husband and me. We have been youth and young adults before – this is our children's first time! The Lord expects us to take

41

the lead in that adjustment because we have more knowledge than they do and where there is more knowledge, more is expected.

When my children are young, I am 90% parent and 10% friend. They need me to be a parent, somebody to establish boundaries and perform so many other tasks. When one of my children becomes an adult, I have spent time and effort in carefully adjusting our relationship until it is 90% friend and only 10% parent. The parent role remains for those crucial moments when my child needs my help, and when my child is drifting off target of eternity.

It is hard for an adult to let relax the parent role and recognize that a child has grown. In my family, it has been hardest for Neil to make the adjustments. When my oldest was 12 years-old, she was invited to go swimming with a friend. Chani and I spent hours choosing a bathing suit and came home with one that was beautiful on her and wonderfully modest. She ran upstairs, changed and came back down carrying her towel. Her dad took one look at her walking down the stairs and promptly ordered her, "Go right back up and put on some clothes!"

I smiled at him and whispered, "Honey, her bathing suit is perfectly modest and in church standards. She looks beautiful!" Neil very quietly whispered back, "When did she get those..." He was completely unprepared for the physical changes in his daughter and even more unprepared for the emotional and social changes that would soon follow. However, he has listened to my suggestions and allowed himself to learn how to be an excellent father of youth and adult children.

Briefly, these are the five stages your child will travel through while learning to communicate in the adult world. Some may start the stages a little late, or have them last longer, or be less obvious as they maneuver through, but these guides should help you pinpoint the needs your youth will have when it comes to socially interacting with adults. If you ignore these stages, pushing the child away or trying to keep them at a younger level of interaction, then a generation gap forms that could last for years. You won't notice it happening at first but by the time your child is 14, the rift will become obvious and almost insurmountable. .

A. At age ten, they begin to hang around, and hover just within ear shot, or they sit quietly in some corner of the adult and teen groups. They are not yet ready to enter into the conversation but they want to hear every bit of it. This is the time when the older people will say, "Why don't you go play?" They are not used to the child hanging around and want to have older conversation without the attentive listening of somebody younger.

B. At age twelve, if the child has been allowed to hang around older conversations, they begin to enter in, usually with humorous or out-of-place statements. They constantly draw attention to themselves. They may be excellent at childhood interaction but in the adult scheme of things, they are completely inept. The hovering phase of learning has passed and they are now making first efforts at developing a skill with all of the errors any novice experiences when learning something new. They seem to have lost a certain amount of thinking ability as they flounder along this trial and error time.

C. At age fourteen, if the youth have been invited into adult interactions, they begin to enter into the conversation with meaningful material. They want to have some serious conversation. Sometimes their views are challenging to the adults. Sometimes their points are not fully thought out. But their emotions are intense and with insight, you can catch glimpses of what these youth will be like as their communication abilities increases.

This is the age where arguments and disagreements increase. This is also where you can really see the consequences of blocking the process of experiencing adult social interaction. If the child has not been invited into adult conversation during the hovering period and again during the inept period, then by the time they hit this challenging stage, they will have decided that adults don't care for their input, and this huge rift is created between the two generations. They retreat from adult circles . . . or at least, their parents' adult circles . Because they think adults perceive them as valueless, they retaliate by making their parents' adult values meaningless. They're completely aware that they'll become adults someday, and when it happens, they feel they'll be too smart to be blind and ignorant like their parents.

D. At age sixteen, the youth want and need social, thoughtful, fun, companionable conversation and interaction with adults. They are only two years away from adulthood, and the ease with which they enter that world depends a great deal on the experiences they've had at home. Allow them to have perspective differences but stand firm if those differences will harm with your child's physical and spiritual safety and effect their eternity. By now, your youth should be able to sit with you and your friends and rarely embarrass you. It is a joy to sit back and watch them express themselves, giving a good view of the sort of peers they will become in a very short time.

If the previous stages have not been encouraged, then this stage gets very secretive. Their emotions are more under control than the 14 year-old. Things seem calmer but in reality, they are moving to accept the rift as a natural way of things and knowing nothing better, expect nothing more.

E. At age eighteen, it is time for the final shift in how you converse with your new adult. It is the parent's job to lead in this transition. They no longer should have to prove themselves *becoming* adults . . . they already are adults and that is never going to change. Now, they only have to prove that they are good adults, and that is entirely their own responsibility. A parent helps in this final transition by the choice of words used in conversation.

In our home, we have had many adults visit over the years. Some have stayed a few nights and some have stayed several months. My children have seen and we have often talked about good adult behavior and responsibility towards others. They know how an adult acts. These discussions take place years before their needed to prepare my children for what to expect as they mature.

When Chamrie turned 18, she asked me, "Mom, can I go to the movies with my friends?" The perfect teaching moment had arrived.

I replied, "Chamrie, say, 'Mom, I'm going to the movies with my friends. I should be home sometime around 12:30."

She got the sweetest, silliest grin on her face and repeated my statement. Now, I still knew where she was and when she would be home. However, she was not asking my permission nor did she have a curfew. She had complete control of her time and actions. Now, I have control of my home and she knows that if she is not keeping the Lord's commandments, she would have to leave.

Every once in a while, I pull a "parent thing" and get frustrated with her. But for the most part, her transition into adulthood has given me a very close daughter, one who calls me just to talk, one who goes out to lunch with me because we're friends, and one who has embraced the Lord's teachings and wishes her other adult friends could love being an adult without resenting their family.

The Last Element of the Living the Homeschool Lifestyle is Managing Attitude

Attitude strengthens communication, supports structure and keeps the fire lit under the purpose of home schooling throughout the years.

How I act and how I feel about myself, my husband, my children and our lifestyle causes me to enjoy life or be miserable. If I am miserable while doing what I know is best for my family then it is time to take control of my attitude. Sometimes this means making adjustments in the structure of our schooling or the management of my time. Often it means gaining an understanding of how my family is interacting with each other. Occasionally it means that I have become lazy and have not been focused on why we are doing this very unusual thing called home schooling. Here are a few things that help keep perspective and joy in the home schooling mother's life.

Relax and enjoy the daily routines. Be amused at the minor conflicts and challenges. You will see them over and over and over. If they drive you insane today and tomorrow and the next day then eventually you will feel that you have lost something. Be quick to laugh and find the bright side of any struggle.

Go out with your husband twice a week. One of those dates could be something as simple as hiding out in the car, whispering on the couch or going shopping. During this time talk about the problems and challenges in the family and evaluate how things are going. Decide to adjust course here and there. Focus on one child at a time as well as the family group. This private date with your companion is a problem-solving time. It isn't very romantic but over the months and years it is just as vital towards a healthy marriage as romance. My favorite time to do this is when Neil is driving because then he can't fall asleep while I talk.

The second date each week should be pure entertainment. It could be romantic, uplifting or just plain fun. We have found that we enjoy this date the most when we go out with other couples. When you are with another couple and the topic of your children and their craziness comes up, it isn't a problem solving situation. Instead, it is a shared moment of "Oh, I guess this is normal if yours do it too." You laugh together over things that might otherwise cause you to grit your teeth. You and your husband get to interact again the way you did when you were single and drawing towards each other amid social contact. It brings out aspects of your personality that sometimes get lost. Renew yourself through these two dates and then renew yourself through personal development.

Set aside one day a week where the children do only private studies, crafts, games or anything self-directed with mild supervision and use that day to study, read, write, pursue a hobby or visit with friends. Do something to satisfy that part of you that is unique. Do this at every week as once a month is simply not enough personal time.

These things, combined with occasional vacations from normal routine, will help you to keep focused on the purpose while enjoying the home schooling process. So my five elements of living the home school lifestyle are:

1. Identifying your purpose.

2. Discovering the philosophies that will help you accomplish your purpose.

3. Establishing the structure that gives shape to your purpose.

4. Understanding family communication to capture learning and magnify relationships.

5. Controlling the attitudes that make this unusual life enjoyable.

The Crowning Joy

Over twenty-four years ago I gave birth to my first child. My little son was so tiny and vulnerable. He was so very innocent and precious. I couldn't be kept away from him.

The day after his birth found Neil and I at the NICU. We were taken into a tiny room to meet with our Marshall's doctor. Very gently, the doctor told us that if our little baby made it through three days, then he would live. He explained that it was important that I take care of myself, that I get the rest I needed, and that while I could spend as much time with my son as I wanted, it would do him little good if I became run down.

Being so new at motherhood and being a young twenty-two-year-old, I followed his traditional advice. Over the next 8 ½ weeks, I visited my son every day but I did so carefully, not wanting to bring about the dreaded curse of overdoing it. I was there when his little heart stopped and the doctor put a needle through his chest to get it beating again. I was there to hold him the one day he miraculously recovered . . . for only a few hours. I was there when they operated on his heart.

But I was not there when his heart stopped another time. I was not there when they put chest tubes through his skin to drain fluid from his lungs and chest cavity. I was not there for 22 hours of his day, every day.

My whole soul longed to be with my baby every minute. I could feel my little one yearning for my presence. Reason yelled at me that it was unnatural to be apart from my young child. But insecurity in my own understanding and trusting in tradition kept me from answering those yearnings. I gave my little angel back into God's hands remembering all the wasted moments when I could have lingered by his bedside and cradled his little head with my hand. A lifetime passed with a loving mother absent more than present.

What is the crowning joy of home schooling? As I gave my oldest daughter over to adulthood, I learned the answer. I have spent my life with my children. They are growing so fast, but I am with them each step of the way. They are not strangers to me. I do not have the intense feeling that they are slipping away, that they have lived a child's lifetime mostly away from me.

I feel an exquisite gratitude for our commitment to live the homeschooling lifestyle. Because of home schooling, my children have a life rich in parental involvement, and I have a life that goes far beyond that of the stereo-typical housewife. I see my children interacting with each other. I see them teach each other. I have watched them enjoying a childhood showered with heavy doses of simple play. I thrill as I see them respecting others and comfortably conversing and interacting with children and adults of all ages and interests. I can see their spirits arising and developing wondrous strengths and fascinating talents. I watch as they discover that struggles are a part of life and nothing to be feared. I hear them talk about their own strengths and weaknesses, recognizing who they are and what is important to them. I hear them talk to adults and peers, easily suggesting ways to improve family life or help other little children. I see a tenderness and patience towards their young brothers and sisters.

As I watched my oldest move into her adult years secure and confident in who she is and pleased with her upbringing, I could not imagine a greater joy for a mother who has dedicated her life to teaching her beloved children – living the homeschool lifestyle over a lifetime – each and every priceless life.

*Cherie Logan and her husband, Dr. Neil C. Logan are the parents of ten children. She began homeschooling in 1985. Cherie has written several books, including the deeply inspirational, **Ten Children Born of Courage and Faith.** Her web site, noblechild.com is dedicated to inspiring mothers in the many aspects of family life and personal development. She lectures at George Wythe College, Colesville Academy and various Homeschool Conferences. Cherie has taught communication skills and goal setting for over 18 years and developed Becoming Crystal Clear, two courses of instruction in using brain language in communication and overcoming blocks to joy, peace and success. She weekly opens her home to local youth through her Noble Child Leadership classes emphasizing intellectual and spiritual development in a highly social setting. Her current passion is teaching the stages youth travel through to become comfortably sociable as adults. Her books can be purchased from classicbooks@accesswest.com.*

I have never let my schooling interfere with my education.

--Mark Twain

Chapter Three
From Sailing to Homeschool

By
Lisa Odaffer

My family lives on a sailboat. Over the past seven years, my husband Jay and I, and our four sons, Alex, Jamie, John and Sam, have traveled by boat from San Francisco, California to the west coast of Florida. Although many other families who live on boats homeschool their children because of constant moves to new and exotic ports of call, we have only changed harbors on average of once every two years or so, mainly because of my husband's work.

We live on the water because we love the boating life. When I met Jay, he was the single dad of seven-year-old Alex. Jay told me, "The best thing about living on a boat was that I can travel the world, and still sleep in my own bed every night!" Even though we haven't done anything to qualify ourselves as world travelers, the continuity of keeping the same home, even as we have had to move from place to place has been a stabilizing influence on the family.

I began my journey into homeschooling in a very unlikely place. I took my first step while still single. Standing with my brand new teaching credential in hand, I was in front of my very own high school classroom.

Hired as a Social Studies and English teacher, I was determined to impart to my students a love of History, Reading and Composition. At my hands they would become productive future citizens with a lifetime love of learning. How naïve I was!

I soon learned the pitfalls of modern public schools. One or two students had the ability to disrupt an entire classroom. I could send them to the office, but I was told in no uncertain terms that if it happened more than once or twice a semester, I was putting my future tenure at risk. Extra time devoted to managing these students in the class deprived the rest of them, and learning suffered. Additionally, my school district had a policy of social passing through the eighth grade.

I was confronted with four classes of ninth graders who had no conception of the connection between the quality of their class work, if it had been turned in at all, and their final grade. There was also a class of eleventh graders who, although they understood the idea in theory, were generally incapable of completing any assignment not collected at the end of the period that it was given. Homework and multi-day assignments (like term papers) were out of the question unless I expected to flunk half the class.

Many of the students had not been academically prepared for high school level work. As products of the Whole Language curriculum, most had never seen a spelling or grammar book and read far below grade level. Since tracking by ability was considered "elitist," the few potentially high achieving children were thrown in with all the rest; it pained me to watch them stagnate and lose interest in the dumbed-down curriculum that the majority of my students required.

At the end of two years I was absolutely discouraged. I was about to give birth to my first baby, a son named Jamie. I decided to take a year off and tackle the problem anew the following year. However, the Lord had something else in mind for me. At the end of that year, I gave birth to another son, John. Alex was attending a private Christian Elementary School with after school care until I could pick him up in the afternoon. A teacher's salary couldn't cover that cost plus day care for two infants, so I regrouped and decided to stay home until both little ones were off to elementary school.

The life of a stay at home mother turned out to be an unexpected blessing for me. My former co-workers warned me that I would be bored stiff and my brain would turn to mush. But they were wrong. I was soon fascinated with my two little boys and pleased with the new relationship I was building with my stepson. I read books on childhood development, read stories to them, played games with them, and watched in awe as they learned and grew. It wasn't long before being home with them changed us from being a "blended family" to a plain old family. Alex was soon calling me "Mom" and the prefix "step-" vanished from our vocabulary forever.

Alex, who had been held back a grade because, you guessed it, he had a hard time learning to read with the Whole Language method, improved at school because he had a Mom to pick him up, chat with the teacher about the day's events and help him get his homework organized and completed every day. I was a little bit uncomfortable about the curriculum that the teacher was using, it didn't seem challenging enough for a child Alex's age. I was also worried about the way the teacher seemed incapable of keeping him in his seat. He didn't seem to have a problem being obedient at home. Occasionally, the teacher would mention that he had a "wandering" problem, but she assured me that he would eventually grow out of it.

I wasn't ready to believe that I could actually know more about my son than the teacher. Even after my experience "inside the system," it's hard to deny the power and prestige of a public school teacher in the eyes of most parents. They seem to know what they are doing, and most of us who may feel uncomfortable are still not so sure. I was sorry later that I didn't follow my earliest instincts.

While trying to cope with how to best help Alex with his school problems, my second son, Jamie, had turned three. I began to notice that he was a bit more active than other children his age. The boy never sat still. He would zip around the room, eagerly investigating anything and everything that caught his eye. He was also a late talker, saying his first sentences at about the same time as his younger brother, John. Days at the park became more stressful, as I was never sure if he would pounce excitedly on another child in an aggressive game, or catch sight of an interesting bird and wander away. Church was a major trial each week. By age four, getting him to sit still for the service was nearly impossible, and I had to stay with him during Sunday school to keep him from crawling under the chairs and pinching the legs of the other children. Other mothers began to gently suggest I have him evaluated for ADHD and get a prescription for Ritalin before sending him off to Kindergarten the following year.

At the same time, Jamie was pestering me to teach him how to read. He understood that words meant something and was impatient to decode them by him. I looked around in the Library and bookstore for some phonics instruction books but all I found were mountains of Whole Language materials.

These were essentially picture books with photos, for example, of things you can find in the kitchen with the name of each item pictured next to it. Students are supposed to look over the pictures and memorize the words, without any conception of how the letters combine to make the sounds. This skill, Whole Language reasons, will come naturally as the child memorizes more and more words. There were also storybooks with lots of pictures. Children are supposed to use the pictures on each page to help them guess any words that they don't already know.

My experience with the poor readers in my high school classes and Alex's struggles in school, because he had taken so long to learn to read, made me wary of using them. The teachers' education courses in college assured us that learning to read was akin to learning to talk or walk. According to their theories, children would pick it up just by being exposed to words and storybooks. Phonics, spelling and grammar were therefore unnecessary. In fact, they claimed that learning individual sounds and practicing sounding out new words over and over turned kids off to learning. If students looked at enough words and pictures, they would just "get it." It sounded great, but I had seen enough of the practical results. I called "Hooked on Phonics" and ordered their reading program instead.

We started by working for fifteen minutes a day and were soon sitting at the table for as long as 45 minutes – a miracle! I discovered that as long as Jamie was really interested in what we were doing, I had his undivided attention. It took six months for him to work his way through level 1. He loved reading words at every opportunity. He devoured the books that came with the program. I wrote more simple phonics stories for him to read to the family.

As Kindergarten crept nearer for Jamie, I was torn. My friends told me I should be glad to be nearly done with my indentured servitude on the Mommy track. They congratulated me for having my children so close together so that I could get back to my "real job" more quickly. I had a bachelor's degree in History with a minor in English, as well as a teacher's credential. I should have been eager to get back to my chosen profession, but I wasn't.

I kept having visions of Jamie terrorizing his future Kindergarten classroom. I knew from experience what one disruptive student could do to the most carefully written lesson plans. I pitied his harried teacher, but I worried about my son more. "Sit down, Jamie! Come here, Jamie! Don't touch that, Jamie! Eyes up front, Jamie! Go to time out, Jamie!" I dreaded the inevitable diagnosis of hyperactivity, and I knew that my smart, active son would soon hate school and have all the love of learning new things driven out of him.

Alex, although improved, was still far from a stellar student. He was actually a very smart boy, but he never really learned to "play school." Although he could easily discuss whatever it was he learned in class, he struggled daily with having the discipline to actually do and turn in his work. He never did grow out of his "wandering" problem, and because his elementary teachers never got serious about dealing with it in any way other than waiting for him to "grow out of it," it was causing a lot of trouble in his middle school classes. I worried that if I went back to work I wouldn't have the time to devote to staying on top of what was going on in his classes. Teaching high school again would also abandon my now 13 year old to an after school program or just an empty boat until the rest of us got home. My heart told me that without supervision he would slide back into homework apathy.

There was also the issue of my growing disillusionment with the current theories of teaching that prevailed in the public elementary schools. Keeping current with the education journals and talking to my friends who were still working convinced me that the new, non-traditional methods were causing more problems than they were solving. How could I go back to teaching other people's children while I was so worried about my own? I was haunted by visions of the disruptive, uninterested, poorly educated boys among my students who had been beyond my ability to really help as well as Alex's lackluster performance. Would that be Jamie's fate?

My husband and I pondered and prayed over what to do for nearly a month. Then with some encouragement from two homeschooling families at church, I tentatively purchased the Calvert Kindergarten curriculum six months before Jamie would have to be enrolled in public school. Even though I wanted to take Alex out of school, too, I was still afraid that I would be biting off more than I could chew. If this turned out to be an absolutely terrible idea, I wouldn't be risking much of Jamie's education by mucking with Kindergarten. But Alex would soon be starting seventh grade, it would be harder to get that back if things didn't work out.

Calvert sounded attractive because it comes with all the necessary books and supplies and has the lesson plans written out for me to use. After all, I knew about high school students, but not a thing about what to teach small children. Calvert gave me the comfort of knowing I wouldn't have to reinvent the wheel. I also got the Pre-K package for John. In six months, I reasoned to myself, I would know whether or not it was working. If all else failed, nothing would be lost and the kids would just start school on schedule.

The boys loved it! It took a few weeks to work out a daily schedule and to decide what subjects I could teach the little boys together (art, science, and music and story time) and what subjects would have to be taught separately (math, phonics and reading). Since we were living on the boat and didn't have the benefit of a backyard for running and playing between lessons, we got memberships to the local zoo and science museum and visited them regularly. I also took them to the YMCA once a week where they could play with other children their age.

By the end of my six-month trial period with the younger two, Alex was flailing around, close to drowning in the seventh grade. The too-easy curriculum of his grade school years in California was finally catching up to him in Middle School, in the far more educationally traditional Alabama. I finally got up the nerve to pull Alex out of school at the end of the third quarter to try to get him back on track.

From the very beginning, I felt as if the windows of heaven had opened and were pouring blessings on our family. To John, who of course had the least amount of math and reading work to do, this was all a great game. For Jamie, it was a revelation. He devoured his workbooks and begged to jump ahead in the pre-written lesson plans. Soon, his attention span had increased significantly enough that his teachers in Sunday School and at the Y asked me what was going on. Once Alex discovered that school could be over quickly or take all day long, depending upon how much time he took and how thoroughly he completed each assignment, he got down to work. Gone were my visions of disaster, replaced by unhurried days spent learning new things.

Adding Alex to the school day required a little more careful planning than my days with only his two younger brothers. I purchased the Calvert eighth grade curriculum package and supplemented it with my own materials from my years as a teacher. The deal was that we would do eighth and ninth grades at home – without taking long breaks for traditional vacations. If all went according to plan, he would start tenth grade with his age group. (Remember, he had been held back in third grade. This would put him back on schedule to graduate with the other kids his age.) At that point he would have the choice of either returning to public school as a high school student or slowly making the transition from homeschooling to local community college courses.

Alex loved the idea of having so much control over his immediate and future destiny. He had long been embarrassed that he was a grade behind in school and was driven to complete the program I had outlined so that he could catch up. He would begin each day with his most difficult subjects, saving the easiest ones for last. We would talk a little about what he needed to do for each lesson and then he would go to his room to get it done. While he was working on his own, I did Jamie and John's lessons at the kitchen table. During this time, I have to admit that Jamie and John had less time to do things like art, music and story time. I focused primarily on reading, math and some cursive writing. But we still had time for one day off the boat at the zoo or museum each week or to take the occasional three-day weekend to go sailing.

Days spent sailing our home, whether in local waters or for longer trips, gave us lots of chances to give the boys an education about the world around them. We would sit in the cockpit and discuss topics like weather, tides, hull displacement, how using ropes and pulleys can help you lift things you couldn't otherwise budge, map reading, marine mammals and navigation by the stars, to name a few. Without TV and videos, I could pop in a book on tape or read short stories while everyone lounged in the sun and enjoyed the day.

Although he is a very active, hands-on father, Jay never felt inclined to get involved in teaching the boys particular lessons. But days on the water and weekends as a family gave him ample opportunity to have long talks with each one of them about how the things he was learning in school applied to the real world. One of my husband's educational pet peeves has always been the way that kids memorize things for a test without ever actually adding to their store of practical knowledge. I have always been thankful that we complement each other in our teaching styles in this way. I can be almost obsessive about following the directions and learning the answers to all of the questions. On the other hand, my wonderful husband has spent many hours showing the boys the world outside their books and worksheets.

That summer, we spent three weeks crossing the Gulf of Mexico en route to our next job in Florida. There was no way that we could have any sort of regular school during those days at sea. The rolling motion of the boat, the number of things to be done while navigating, and turns taken steering made it too difficult to concentrate on a textbook for very long. We counted dolphins, read novels and just talked about everything under the sun. There's nothing wrong with taking some time off from the steady drumbeat of Math, Science, English and History to enjoy some time together as a family.

We arrived in Florida just as school was starting and Alex was the right age to start ninth grade. I was concerned about finding a way for him to make new friends in the area and so I encouraged him to sign up for the high school marching band. Florida, which is very homeschool friendly, allows homeschoolers to sign up for individual classes at the high school. Besides having music for first period every day (freeing my morning for more time with his little brothers), after school marching practices gave him a reason to be more disciplined about getting his work done on time.

By the end of that school year our 18-month program had brought him through ninth grade. He was having so much fun with his friends and activities in Band that he decided he wanted to enroll full time at the public high school the following year. It was a little awkward for him to get used to having school five days a week again, with no flexibility on days that he didn't feel like doing his best, but he wanted to be there, so he got himself into the routine.

In the 18 months that he spent at home with me, I learned that he never really had a problem understanding and analyzing information that he got by participating in classroom discussions, but that the textbooks weren't doing him a bit of good. His real weakness was a lack of "school skills." So, I was able to work with him in a way that a classroom teacher couldn't to improve his writing and reading levels so that he would be able to do grade appropriate work. Plus, in our one-on-one situation he learned that he couldn't just make up excuses and avoid turning in assignments. By having me in direct control of immediate consequences for not doing his work, he soon learned that it was just easier to stop goofing around and get it over with. With these skills in hand, he returned to public school (and the social life he had been craving) at age 15, much more capable of success.

Currently, Jamie (now age 6) and John (age 5) are in Calvert's grades two and one, respectively. I am also still using the lessons from my original investment in Hooked on Phonics to reinforce their reading skills. I'm aware that many homeschooling families find Calvert too structured, but it seems to fit the personalities of the children. I appreciate not having to spend hours outside of teaching on preparation time and we are happy with the traditional methods and excellent results.

The two little boys and I begin our day at about 8 am. We have breakfast while I check e-mail and read my favorite lists and newsgroups on the Internet. At 9 am we start school with prayer. John likes to go first so Jamie has free time to read, do puzzles or play quietly while John does his math, phonics and reading. Then John has free time while Jamie does the same three subjects at his level. We break for lunch at noon. After lunch the boys do cursive practice together, followed by either science or art. The school day is generally over by 1:30 or 2 pm.

While both boys are very active, gone are the days when I worried that Jamie would never be able to control acting out on his every whim. When his attention starts to waver, I have the power to stop the offending distraction, end a slow moving lesson, or allow him to skip ahead to something new. As long as he is interested in what we are doing, he will sit at the table and work eagerly. The results have transferred to the rest of his days, as well. He will now sit through church with a story or workbook on his lap, plays more appropriately with his peers, and remembers rules like "don't leave the playground," and "stay next to Mommy in the store." Some days are wilder than others, but overall, there is no denying the positive change in him.

The local school district requires 180 days of school per year, and the Calvert curriculum provides 160 lessons. The extra twenty days give us the freedom to stretch out lessons that the boys may find difficult or especially interesting, and gives me the ability to incorporate trips to the library, zoo or historical park, or to do things like take the tour at a local farm or plant.

I've never been in love with two and a half months of summer vacation. Even as a child, I remember being bored in the summer more than anything else, and as a teacher it was plain to me that the students forget much of what they have learned in the previous grade. So I generally stretch our 180 days out over the entire year. It's pretty rare for us to do school every day for a whole week. Instead, we work three or four days and then take a day off for household chores and play. That keeps us very laid back and relaxed. School breaks of more than a day or two are scheduled around visits by Grandma, holidays like Easter or Christmas, and family vacations.

Every day, when Dad gets home, the boys all take turns telling him about their day. Alex will tell a funny story about something that happened in one of his classes or show off a returned test. Each of the younger brothers pulls out his best worksheet of the day or the latest story from his reader. Daddy understands that his encouragement and approval mean the world to the sons who want to grow up to be just like him.

Having recently given birth to my fourth child, Sam, I can't imagine doing anything differently. I have never done anything more personally fulfilling in my life. Nothing can compare to the experience of watching your child learn and grow. And they are all the better for having a teacher that can give her undivided attention and loves them more than anything else in the world.

I suppose that it was inevitable that I've lost touch with most of my teaching friends. In the end, they've remained loyal to the public school Establishment and can't see what I can possibly gain by dropping out of the career world and choosing to teach my kids at home. While to me it seems perfectly natural that my family is now the center of my life. I am surrounded by my rewards every day. Alex is bringing home his first good report cards ever. This afternoon, Jamie is lying on the living room floor working on a geography puzzle book and John is drawing me a picture of Spiderman. "Do you know what Spiderman is saying, Mommy?" he asks. "He is saying 'I love you!'"

Lisa Odaffer: lives with her family on their 45 foot sailboat, Blue Heaven. They have sailed throughout the Gulf Coast of the United States and are currently making preparations to take an extended Home School field trip in the Caribbean. She has written several non-fiction articles and short stories about sailing with children, home schooling, and family life.

Education is not the filling of a pail,

but the lighting of a fire.

--William Butler Yeats

Chapter Four
Progressive Mastery Education

By
Gail Thomas

When people meet my children, no one comments on how well they do their math. They do notice how they act, how they treat each other and how they respond to me. The goal of our homeschool efforts is to produce people who can build a life for themselves. We would like them to be people who reflect our values and beliefs but more importantly we want to raise them to have values and beliefs.

My husband and I sat down and figured out what we felt was important to give our children to prepare them for life and the possibility of college. It is important to note, that we are trying to open opportunity for them, not shut off any options and so preparation for college is a part of our plan. This list became our graduation requirements. Laws vary from state to state and you should start with a good understanding of what will meet your own state's requirements. Let me stress-- these are our family's ideas of what we want to require. You sit down as a family, decide where you are going then; plan how to get there.

Since my husband is an engineer, he felt that it was important for them to have good math skills. We knew they would need to be able to read well enough to function and write well enough to be understood. I wanted them to have an overview of world history, to understand where we have been as a nation. I also wanted them to understand how the world works so science was added. We also believe they need an over view of the bible and, (again this is for our kids) to understand our faith. Our ultimate goal is to teach them to think and to learn.

We broke down the amount of time we had to raise them into five parts.

1. <u>Rejoice! 1st year</u>

2. <u>Relationship stage: ages 2y-5y</u>

3. <u>Ready stage: Ages 6-10 (1st -4th grade</u>)

4. <u>Receive stage: Ages 11-13 (5th- 8th grade</u>)

5. <u>Respond stage: Ages 14-18 (9th - 12th</u>)

I'll explain each one of those for you and tell you our goals.

Rejoice! Stage: First year of life

This stage actually starts before a birth in the way we prepare the other children for the new baby. It is our attitude that the new baby is not just my baby or even Mommy and Daddy's baby, but everyone's new baby. This amazing gift is given to us as a family. I become the mother of an additional child, but the youngest child takes on a new role all together. For the first time they become a big brother or sister. Children are a tremendous blessing- we act on that belief as we joyfully prepare to receive a new child into our family circle.

While most of us pack a bag for the hospital, we also pack a picnic basket. The children use a check list to load it up with disposable plates, forks, disposable champagne glasses, sparkling cider... everything necessary to celebrate a birthday except the cake. Then they make "Welcome" cards for our little bundle. Younger children sometimes draw pictures. Charlie's contribution is taking a picture of everyone to be included. After the baby has arrived, Charlie takes the youngest child to the bakery to select a baby cake. Our bakery carries a very small size that looks like the very top layer of a wedding cake. Then as soon as it is practical, all the children come to the hospital to meet our new child.

The "Welcome cards" ritual took on very special meaning when our Allie was born. She had some difficulty at birth and couldn't attend her party when her siblings came up to the hospital. I went in the NICU and placed the sweet messages in her isolet along with the picture of all the children who were praying for her and waiting for her come home. When the nurse helped me to roll her to the window, they saw all their warm wishes surrounding her. I was able to tell them how encouraging it was to me when I would go in to hold her or nurse her. (it also encouraged the nurses who were taking care of her.) When she still wasn't ready to leave the hospital when I was discharged it helped our family feel connected to her.

Today, as I write this, Allie is a beautiful, happy and healthy five-year-old. My grandmother says she is the only one of the seven who is anything like me, and she is just like me. I tried not to notice the mildly amused look in my sweet grandmother's eye. I'm sure she meant that as a compliment, really.

There is anther thing we do during this stage which is a little unique. I speak for the baby. When a young sibling is holding the new baby and the baby smiles, I will often say "Oh! Look how she loves her big brother!" I have been criticized for this. How do I know what the baby is thinking? My response is always the same. By the time the baby is old enough to complain, the relationship will already be defined as a loving supportive one. The older sibling (and we are usually talking about the under five crowd) will accept that the child loves him, and is looking up to him as an example. And we have moved on to the next phase: Relationship.

Relationship stage: Ages 2 - 5

This phase establishes the culture of our home. What we will allow and what we won't. One of the most important things we require is obedience. I work with them from the time they are able to respond to requests by playing little games with them.

Even our youngest toddlers learn to obey by playing with me. I roll them a ball, and say, "Bring it back to Mommy." When they do, they get smothered in kisses, hugs and praise. A favorite game is "Go find the sibling." I will tell them go find a certain sibling. When the baby finds the brother or sister gets smothered with kisses and hugs. (As a side benefit, it is quite encouraging to have a happy little one seek you out, be happy to find you and then plant an excited kiss on you. Many of these game times have ended with most of the children coming to see what the baby is up to and result in some of our happiest family memories.

We also ask our toddlers to throw away small things when it is appropriate. I try to put a small basket in their playpen that is big enough to hold a few toys and have then put the toys back in the basket before they get out of the playpen. Of course if they are upset or crying I don't require it. These are just little games, and like any game it should be fun for the child.

Once they obey and cooperate as a general rule, and by this I mean without serious resistance, I potty train them. This happens for different children at different ages. If you try to potty train a child before you have taught them to obey and cooperate, you will have a tough time. You really need to gain their cooperation before the age of two, or you will have a much harder time gaining it at all.

During this time, you toddler naturally wants to be with you. Take advantage of this window of opportunity. Make them responsible for helping you during chore time. In this way, you can train them to do various chores and pass along a good attitude about working hard.

This phase lasts until about the age of five. Academically, if they want to learn to write their name, teach them, but don't force it! My advice? Read, read, read, read..... and then read some more. Read out loud while they play quietly nearby. Cuddle in your bed after bath time with a good book. Listen to books on tape in the car. Use books as a reward for good behavior or a new skill learned. Begin to get them to tell you about their day. This skill will be invaluable to them as they begin to organize their own thoughts and write later.

Ready Stage: Ages 6 to 10 (1st - 4th grade)

During this phase, concentrate on teaching your child to read. It is by far the most important skill they will ever learn. It opens up the entire world to them! Once they have a new skill, they must use it everyday. We keep a reading list for each child.

Show them how to write. Let them copy words from the paper, magazines, even cereal boxes. Anything that interests them. Show them how to make the letters properly.

We use Ruth Beechik's "Early start in Arithmetic." as a guideline for math activities at this stage. We use board games, card games and dominoes. We count real things. We sort socks and set the table. I love computer games that reinforce skills. We drill with flash cards all the math facts they have learned, both addition and subtraction.

During this phase we take long walks, go to interesting places and read interesting things. We go to the library every week and teach them how to choose good books. We teach them to work and be responsible by assigning them daily chores. We pass on our faith through the celebration of holidays, teaching them the children's catechism and family devotions most evenings.

At the beginning of the 4th school year, I teach them the multiplication tables, all of them. This is an important tool, even if it is only for the next eight years of school. For my children, it gives them a real sense of accomplishment and shows me that they are ready to move on to the Receive Stage (5th -8th grades).

Receive Stage: Ages 11 to 13 (5th-8th grade)

We chose Saxon Math. We start them in Saxon 54 and skip the first 40 lessons in successive books (since it is review anyway; this will enable them to do well on their SATS). Our kids continue into Advanced Math and Calculus. This will obviously continue into the next learning stage. We use flashcards to review, not learn, math facts.

We concentrate on spelling and grammar at this stage. We introduce Latin and Spanish. We continue to explore the world together including every part of science imaginable. We do gooey experiments and read the biographies of great scientists. We give them a foundation in the science behind Creation Science.

We study History by breaking it into 4 parts, and cover one per year. We also make use of a notebook timeline so that they can see History unfold and see the influences of other fields (like science and technology) effect History. In the first year we begin with Ancient Civilizations. In the second year we cover the Roman Empire through the Reformation. In the third year we proceed through the Explorers. Lastly, in the fourth year, we cover the founding of our country and study modern history through the prism of our Christian world view.

Once my children are comfortable writing (usually after they can read well, write legibly and can spell fairly well) we require them to write everyday. During this stage most of their actual learning takes place. They are becoming increasingly independent and ready for the next stage.

The Respond Stage: Ages 14 - 18 (9th - 12th grade)

Since we school all year, my children finish Saxon Math by the 10th grade. We continue by reviewing Math with Standard Deviants DVDs. Now Science moves to the forefront in a more formal way. We use Dr Jay Wile's Physical Science, Biology, Chemistry, and Physics.

History is used as a framework at this stage and the student begins reading twenty-five books written in each time period per year. They don't read about Plato, they read Plato's actual writings. They continue to plot these things on their timelines and can see the context under which these things were written. You can pare down the number of books, it is important however that the read representative pieces from all across history not merely books about history.

It is important to our family that our children grasp Bible history as well. We use Dr. RC Sproul's "Dust to Glory" video series. It covers the span of scripture from Genesis through Revelation. Dr Sproul happens to belong to our denomination, but you can substitute something else here.

We like for our children to study Logic, but do not require it for all. We do require that they use their time wisely. We encourage apprenticeships and volunteer jobs. It is important that they realize our responsibilities do not end at our driveway.

At every stage expose them to music and the arts. Let them participate as they choose. Some families opt for classes, others buy art supplies. Let them pick up an instrument. We require that our children stick with it for three months as a minimum. When they choose a book we require that they read at least three chapters before giving it up.

In every stage let them explore their interests, computer, and sports (although we have found organized sports too time demanding). Watch superior TV or none at all. Read out loud. Listen to books on tape. Allow your children to develop special interests and spend time on them.

We require that they choose a language to study after Latin and Spanish. If they are undecided, they continue in Spanish. We prepare for the SATs/ ACT aggressively and encourage them to take CLEP tests and receive both high school and college credit.

That is a lot to cram into about eighteen years. Basically it is:

Rejoice! Babyhood -talk to them, read to them, and enjoy them!

Relationship: Establish the culture in your home. Main goal: obedience.

Ready: Natural learning phase. Our Unschool-ey time. Main goal : reading, handwriting

Receive: Nail down the basics. (grammar, spelling, math...)

Respond: Expand basic knowledge and move into advanced knowledge. During this phase, prepare for college and for life.

Gail Thomas: Gail and her husband Charlie live with their children in Opelika, Alabama. This past year, their oldest child , Caleb, graduated from high school and is currently pursuing a career in filmmaking. His first short film, "Space Available" placed third in the high school division of the Movie Gallery's International Film Competition (the only homeschooler to be a finalist). You can keep up with his work at his web site www.code37films.com. Gail also has a website at www.ffoj.com.

An education isn't how much you

have committed to memory,

or even how much you know.

It's being able to differentiate

between what you know and what you don't.

--Anatole France

Chapter Five
I Am the Perfect Educator

Avoiding Burnout
By
Donna Knox

I am the Perfect Home Educator

As a veteran home educator and mother to nine children, parents often ask me for advice and guidelines for setting up their school year. I meet folks from all walks of life with so many perspectives on learning. Some want the full 'school at home' structure and others are more relaxed, but I have found that most are somewhere in between. And many times those who want a lot of structure relax after the first or second year as they see their children learning amazing things and how they want to know information.

Over the years I have thought about this concept we call "learning". I have seen that throughout the early years of a child's life parents have great confidence that they will teach their child to walk, talk, eat with a fork, tie a shoe, use a toilet, drink from a cup, walk up stairs and even write their name. But for some reason when a child reaches about six, parents lose that confidence and begin relying on people-"experts"- who proclaim to know many things concerning "all" children. These same experts of course will change their theories many times during their lifetime without ever looking back to the children and the damage done.

Why would we want to ignore our inborn instinctual and natural desire to guide and teach our own children? Why do we no longer believe our children want to learn when they turn seven and we are told it's time for "real" school as if what we had been doing for seven years is NOT real?

Remember when they begged to wash dishes? To learn how to scrub the tub? To learn to write their name? To help cook? To learn to count money to buy candy? And we, their parents, just very simply in our daily walk provided them the answers and taught them the skills. We saw the interest and guided them. They were eager to learn and we were eager and confident in our ability to teach them. Why the change at seven? Why is it we as parents no longer see ourselves as smart enough to teach them to add? Or to read or to learn a noun or a pronoun? Is this small amount of information in the big scheme of life so hard to teach? Or learn? Or is it that we have allowed ourselves to believe the misguided conception that parents are just not qualified to teach anything except what the experts allow and bless And that children don't want to learn from their parents anyway?

In general, homeschoolers have rejected these ideas by refusing to give the responsibility of teaching their children to anyone else....or have we?

If getting through a chapter, test or book on history is more important then a child wanting to learn about stars, are we really "teaching" them? If it's more important to stay on "track" according to grade level, than it is to spend a year exploring the state, have we set our own standards in learning based on our own family or some artificial structure? Furthermore, if we rely on someone out there to tell us what and how our children learn without ever watching them to see what they are ready to learn, aren't we still dependent on someone who doesn't know our children?

No book or curriculum or teacher knows your child or your family well enough to presume to tell you what/how/when to teach them anything. Parents ARE the experts on THEIR children. We can glean from others, we can watch families and we can read books, but the minute we allow THEM to make us do certain things, we have succumbed to allowing someone else to "teach" our children.

I don't have a set method I use and I rarely give myself a label such as unschooler or eclectic or even homeschooler. I just consider myself a parent and view learning as an integral woven aspect of our daily life. Sometimes we use books, sometimes we use conversation and sometimes we simply learn in ways unknown even to me.

Listen to our children. Watch them play. Converse on things from "why is water wet" to "Whether scarab beetles eat people from the inside out" to "are all Nazis evil?" to "is baking soda and baking powder the same?". All day our children give us many opportunities to teach them on THEIR level of maturity, interest and desire. This is the ultimate giving to your child, to your family and years later to your grandchildren.

I will tell people who think with nine children and twenty years of homeschooling that I have it all together and know all the great homeschooling secrets that YES!! I am an expert in homeschooling….."MY" children. I am the perfect mom....for "MY" children. I am the most organized Structured Teacher....for" OUR" family. Here's my secret: I don't teach. My children learn in spite of the fact that I am not the "expert" for anyone but them.

Avoiding Burnout

Over the years, I have spoken at many educational seminars and talked to veteran homeschoolers. One concern that I have heard again and again is how to avoid feeling overwhelmed and stressed out. Many mothers find themselves feeling tired with the hours spent on making children do all their work, setting up academic schedules, and being involved in many extra curricular activities.

Learning is a lifelong process and, as independent thinkers we strive to find methods and resources to help our children learn in ways that best suit them. We understand the value of education for our children. Often, parents will begin homeschooling their children with traditional textbooks and all the accompanying "help". As a parent's level of confidence in their own abilities increases, a strictly traditional textbook schedule can add stress to a family's life. Sometimes it takes a while to figure out what the problem is. How a parent responds varies one can blame the child or one can blame the method and curricula.

Recognizing these overwhelming feelings is the first key to resolution. The second key is solving them. After much thought on this, I have come up with a few things that can be of some help.

1. Take time to communicate with your children. If your child has spent time in the public schools, it is easy to forget how to really listen to them. They want to tell you what they would

like to do, in what areas they are interested, and where they would like to go with their interest. Sit down, listen to them, and talk to them. You will learn amazing things about their thought process as well as what things they are capable of doing.

2. Focus in on your child's learning styles, interests, abilities, maturity level as well as your learning styles. Even though education is often defined by grade levels and then learning assigned according to those levels, there is no reason to believe it is helpful or needful by your child. Neither is it a worthwhile goal for your child. Many areas come into play for a child to "learn," especially when dealing with abstract ideas and concepts. If a child is a visual learner yet you learn with auditory skills, you may naturally choose resources that appeal to you but quickly become frustrating to your child.

3. Choose curricula/books carefully, if at all. You will find that the more money you spend on books, the more pressure you will feel to complete every page and chapter. Before investing a lot of money, buy one or two books and make sure your child is able to use them and likes them. I have known parents who have bought an entire computer-based grade-level curriculum only to discover their child hated it because they could not take

books with them on trips or lounge on the bed to read. Textbooks should be used as references and not as the only source of information.

4. Grade-level books can be misleading and detrimental to learning. There is no such thing as grade-level information. This is a myth invented and perpetuated by a system that needs ways to monitor, grade, and label children. Information is simply information, and giving children access to knowledge will insure they learn at their own rate rather then being forced to keep up with or slow down to a rate predetermined by someone else.

5. The actual 12 years of school can be completed in about 6 years. If we don't hurry a child at a young age but allow them time to mature in all areas, we can be assured that they will learn everything they need to at the right time. His or her timetable is different than any other child's. School does not need to be broken up in twelve years. Children can do many different levels at once. So much time is spent in public school as review. When you remove that element, you have a streamlined method of learning.

6.   Take planned and unplanned breaks. A day away from the norm will do wonders in invigorating a child as well as the parent. Going to a museum, a park, or even just out to lunch can help a child internalize ideas and thoughts. Often when a child is struggling with a concept, taking a break will help them get past stumbling blocks, internalize new concepts and skills, or give them time to think about what is being asked of them. Learning is a very personal endeavor, and we need to give children space to learn. It can also be times of personal growth for the parent as they learn to trust their children.

7.   There is no magical key to learning. No on invented knowledge. It simply is there for the taking. If one person can learn something, anyone can with motivation, interest, and maturity. To think that only experts can teach children is to suggest that information is sacred and not available to everyone either online or at a library.

8.   Catch those windows of learning. By listening to our children on a daily basis, we can take advantage of these learning windows. Knowing what they are interested in gives us opportunities to find the resources needed to help our children.

9.   Don't borrow trouble from tomorrow. If your child is only five years old, don't worry about college. By that time, things will be different than now. Don't even worry about next year; concentrate on today. Tomorrow will be here soon enough.

10. Resist the urge to make book learning/academic time REAL learning and all of life NOT real learning. Book learning is not more important than non-book learning. If we give the impression that "real" school is when you are working in books and playtime is all other times, we rob our children of developing a learning attitude that all of life is education. All of life is here for us to learn from, both from our mistakes and our triumphs.

11. Commitment to your child. Home education is a lifestyle, NOT an option. If we commit ourselves to educating our children through thick and thin, through stressful times as well as fun times, without the option of going to pubic school, we will finish the course we set out to do raise happy, competent, well-balanced children. We ourselves will learn how to creatively solve problems and our children will see how it is done. They themselves will learn that you don't throw in the towel as the hint of a tough situation, but you work with all parties involved to find a solution. Putting children back into school simply tells they are not as important as they should be.

12. Point out your interests. Allow the child to see what you are interested in rather than trying to tell a child what they should like. Letting them see you get excited about life helps them develop an excitement also.

The bottom line is, "What do we believe about home education?" If we believe that we, as parents, are responsible to clothe, feed, and nurture our children, then educating them must also be on that list. It is not something we should give to the government to do simply because we are told it is for the best. The frustrations and stresses we will feel are parental issues, not educational issues. If you are committed to home education for you family, you will work through those issues without resorting to putting the child back into public school or worse yet, blaming the child for the problems rather than the materials or our expectations.

Although these ideas won't promise a non-stressful, non-foot-stomping, or always-smooth sailing day of home schooling, it will help you think through those times when home education seems akin to teeth pulling. It will help you put into perspective what is really important and worth your time, energy, and love.

Donna Knox is a mom of 9 children who have never been exposed to government institutes of education. She is the administrator of Dayspring Academy, a legal covering for home educators in Alabama and a community midwife.

A fool's brain digests philosophy into folly,

science into superstition, and

art into pedantry. Hence university education.

George Bernard Shaw

Chapter Six
Unschooling The Teen Years

Time Management

By
Karen Gibson

Unschooling The Teen Years

Our Journey to Homeschooling

Our family's unschooling adventure officially began eight years ago, although I feel that my husband and I have been unschoolers for at least all of our adult lives. As adults, there were many things we discovered we needed to know that we had not learned in school. Most certainly I experienced unschooling first-hand when I became a mother as I learned to adjust and cope with parenthood. We had three children within a five-year time span, a daughter and two sons, and even when they were very young, I was amazed at the differences in their personalities and their needs. As it usually does when young children are involved, the topic of preschool came up now and then from well-meaning friends and family. We lived on a farm and they were worried that our children would not be adequately socialized or prepared for Kindergarten. But I was not willing to allow someone else a say in how they were raised, nor let someone else enjoy more of those early years with my children than I would be able to if they were placed in preschool. I also could not comprehend why it should be necessary to have someone else introduce my children to the world, when I knew I could do just as well at home. After all, that's what those preschool years are all about, children learning about themselves and their place in the world. How could someone else be better at that than I?

When it was time for our eldest to go to Kindergarten, though, I never considered that there might be any other options. I had never heard of homeschool, and even if I had, I doubt I would have thought twice about it. It was just a given that our children would attend the same small rural school that my husband had attended. And, for the most part, it was a fine school. Our eldest adapted quite nicely and grew to love school. Our middle child was another story. Even at Kindergarten he was not happy with the amount of busy work he felt he had to do, things like cutting and pasting, when he really wanted to learn more about science! But, all in all, our experience at that public school was such that, if we had not moved to another state and experienced another school system, our children probably would have never experienced the freedom of homeshooling.

The summer before our eldest child's fifth grade year we moved across the country and all three children were enrolled in the local public school. It was small school where everyone knew everyone, very similar to the school district we had left behind, or so we thought. We were unprepared for the difference in culture and attitude at the new school, unprepared for the lack of emphasis on academics, and unprepared for atmosphere of corporal punishment, to name just a few of the reasons we became displeased with the local public school system. After a few short months, the changes had overwhelmed our eldest child to the point where she was requesting to be homeschooled and she was continually physically ill from the stress of going to school. And so, at the end of that school year and after a lot of research on homeschooling, we decided to try homeschooling for a year to see how it went.

While there were several reasons we withdrew our children from the public school system, and those reasons were different for each child, the reasons we continued to homeschool after the first year were few. First, we had come to fully realize that, in order for our children to succeed in the public school system, they had had to subsume their natural learning desires and their innate areas of strength to fit within the system's "one size fits all" mold. And second, we had discovered just how much the public school system, with its structure and schedules and pressures and demands, had totally consumed our family life. We now knew just how liberating and intoxicating it could be to learn what you wanted, the way you wanted, and when you wanted, and there was no way we could turn the clock back from that knowledge.

An Unschool Beginning

When we first began to homeschool, we followed the paradigm with which we were familiar, re-creating school at home. Within a few short months, though, I was experiencing what many first-time homeschoolers experience when they attempt school-at-home homeschooling: burnout! Not only were the children dissatisfied with what they were learning, but I felt very stressed by trying to cover three different grade levels of material. Surely there had to be a better way? So in December I declared a vacation from "school" and researched more on homeschooling. I read about learning styles and began to realize that my learning styles were distinctly different from those of my children. The resources I was using to teach worked well for me as a teacher, but were not what best suited my children for learning. And then I discovered that there were many other methods of homeschooling besides "school at home." That was when I first came across the term "unschooling," which sounded more like "return to sanity" to me. It was obvious to me upon reading about unschooling, child-led and interest-led learning, that this was the way my husband and I naturally learned best. If unschooling worked for us, then why not for our children?

One of the first books I read while researching unschooling was Grace Llewellyn's *Teenage Liberation Handbook.* Prior to reading her book, I had never thought about the diverse ways one could study a particular subject or learn a skill. Unschooling maintains that learning takes place everywhere in everyday life, but until you experience unschooling yourself and see it's successes over time, it is very easy to be a doubting Thomas. Sure, you can learn something on your own, but is that "legitimate" learning? Is it the same quality of learning as someone teaching you or having a book to guide you? My research on learning styles and my own observations of certain family members had shown me that many people learn best by simply doing, by experiencing something at the most basic, hands-on level. Was the knowledge learned any less useful or real simply because it was not learned in a class? I realized that I had been confining my thinking to the public school "in the box" mentality. Llewellyn's book quite literally opened up a whole new exciting world of possible avenues for gaining an education. Other authors I found tremendously helpful and informative were John Taylor Gatto, John Holt, Mary Griffith, and Raymond & Dorothy Moore.

As I was discovering unschooling in theory, our two youngest children were putting it into practice. During our so-called "vacation," they were continuing to explore and learn using the computer software, books, and other gifts they had received for Christmas. I could see that they really didn't need me to direct their learning; they were quite capable of pursuing knowledge on their own!

Unfortunately, our eldest child did not seem to adjust as well as the two youngest. She was unable to think of any subject she wanted to study or even anything she wanted to do, preferring to wait for some authority figure to tell her what to study next. Several long-time homeschoolers told me this was what she had learned in public school, to wait for someone to tell her what to do next, to wait for the bell to ring, to ignore her own interests and desires. They then explained that she needed a period of deschooling, a period of time to rest and recover from public school and rediscover herself and her needs and desires. And they were right! After several months of de-schooling, when she did little more than sleep, read "fluff" books, and watch television, her natural curiosity was awakened and she no longer needed someone to direct or control her learning.

Unschooling the Elementary Years

Eight years ago unschooling was still a mostly unknown term to homeschoolers. If you had access to the Internet you might have come across the term, but otherwise the closest you might have heard were "relaxed," "eclectic," or possibly "delight-driven." Today almost all homeschoolers have heard of unschooling, but many still are unsure how it actually works. Or, they might grudgingly allow that unschooling could work with very motivated children, or perhaps for grade-school age children (once they have been taught to read and, of course, still accomplish a daily amount of written and/or math work). But unschooling high school? Surely a child must get serious during the high school years in order to accomplish what they will need for college acceptance! Surely unschooling must come to a screeching halt by eighth or ninth grade!

It is easy to understand how unschooling works during the grade school years. After all, the reality of unschooling in practice is not that much different from unit studies when you examine it closely. For example, a child follows one interest intensely for a period of time and during the course of that interest he can eventually cover almost every academic subject area. In our case, the interest was basketball, the child was our youngest, Charles, and the duration was about three years (from about the age of seven to ten). If it did not have to do with basketball, Charles did not want to worry about it. And yet, the areas that he did cover and learn about through his interest in basketball were amazing. They included:

- Geography - Charles could show you on a United States map where every NBA team was located. He researched other large cities in North American to decide which might next possibly gain a NBA Team. He could point out on a world map all the countries that had basketball teams participating in the 2000 Summer Olympics. In addition, he researched each country in order to create mascots and pennants based upon that country's specific geography, animals, flags or principle product.

- Reading - If the book or magazine or article or website had to do with basketball, Charles wanted to read it.

- Writing - Charles always was writing about basketball, including making charts and schedules and imaginary game news articles.

- Math - Sports involve a lot of math, including player and team statistics, win/loss records, etc. Basketball was no exception.

- Science - Sports are nothing more than the principles of physics in action. Observing and understanding how these forces worked gave Charles a deeper understanding of the physical world.

- History - Even a sport has a history, and basketball was no exception. By reading about the players and the history of the sport, discussions naturally led to other things that were occurring in the world at the same time. Other topics that also came up were race relations and civil rights, and the start of women's basketball.

This is just a sampling of the things that Charles learned by pursuing what to me seemed like an almost obsessive interest in basketball. Other areas included advertising and marketing, computer skills, research skills, setting personal goals and other life skills, and much more. So while I might have worried that his passion for basketball was distracting him from his "schooling," I instead saw that learning was occurring through his interest in basketball. And while he did not acquire knowledge quite the way I would have mapped out, the end result was really what counted. It has been my observation that knowledge acquired through one's own interests rather than the dictates and demands of others is knowledge gained for a lifetime.

Unschooling the High School Years

So what about the high school years? Can unschooling still work then? Can a child prepare for a career or college simply by following his/her interests? Our family is currently navigating through those high school years, so the verdict is still up in the air for us, but we are certainly attempting it. And what we have discovered so far is that as each of our children have approached high school and adulthood, they have done so with different goals in mind, different approaches, and different interpretations of what "success" will mean for them. Each is creating his/her own individual pathway to adulthood.

Our daughter Kat, nineteen, graduated in 2003 and was just recently married. She always stated that she did not want to go to college simply to go. She preferred to really begin her life, find a job, maybe travel a bit, and then, when she finally decided what she might want to go to college for, she would enroll. And so far, that is just what she is doing, working full-time and successfully living on her own. While in high school she took several dual-enrollment classes at local community colleges (a program offered here in Alabama) that awarded her both high school and college credits. She took only classes that intrigued her and did very well in them. She also refused to study subjects at home that did not interest her, such as geometry or chemistry. She was fairly certain she would not be going into a field that required such classes and since she had no interest in them, she refused to study them. Instead, she followed her interests and her high school transcript shows that with such diverse credits as Celtic History, Aviation History, Civil Air Patrol Cadet Program, Martial Arts, History of Religion, Computer Graphic, HTML Web, Shakespeare, Photography, Economics, and Conceptual Physics. All of these subjects were studied on her own, through no formal class and with no formal curricula. In fact, the only subjects that she studied in the more traditional, textbook fashion were those that she took through the dual-enrollment program at the community college (Sociology, Western Civilization, Spanish, and Accounting). Everything else was self-taught through a variety of resources and hands-on experiences, both at home and in the community. Her high school transcript consisted of over twenty-four credits, only two of those being the dual-enrollment classes.

Kat accomplished a good, even slightly above-average score on her SAT test in her senior year, even without credits in those more mainstream math and science subjects. Yes, she could have scored higher if she had studied more mathematics, but that was not important to her and her goals. In fact, the only reason she took the SAT at all was that the colleges here required her SAT scores in order to award her college credit for those dual-enrollment classes she had taken. And, if she did decide to enter college within the next few years, the local colleges would still want an SAT or ACT score for entry. So she made the decision to take the test, but it really did not matter to her much what score she got, as long as it was high enough to ensure entry whenever, if ever, she decided to apply to any college.

As non-traditional as Kat's high school journey was, our son David's is proving to be slightly more structured, but still true to our unschooling ideals. David is sixteen and not really sure what career he wants, although game programming has always intrigued him. Whatever he eventually decides upon, he is pretty sure it will have to do with science and computers. Up until this past year, he has done very little formal academics. We have read history (*A History of US* by Joy Hakim, along with various works for world and American history), and classics together (we are just finishing up *The Three Musketeers* by Alexander Dumas). He has met with a tutor for the past year and a half, learning C++ computer programming and creating his own computer game. He has explored a great deal of algebra and geometry to satisfy his curiosity and for information needed for computer programming. He has also studied a variety of science resources (magazines, books, videos, software, etc.) in many areas, including genetics, biology, physics, geology, astronomy, chemistry, etc. Last fall David thought he might want to go to MIT for college, so we explored the MIT website and talked to their recruiter to discover exactly what they require for admission and whether they require anything additional from homeschoolers. What we discovered was that, while the subjects they require is pretty standard, there is no requirement in the way that they are covered.

Now that David is fairly certain the direction he wants to move in, though, we are covering a few subjects in a bit more structured fashion. He is working through math texts to cover the necessary math courses (currently working through Harold Jacob's *Elementary Algebra*). Since a foreign language was required by MIT and Latin has always intrigued David, we have begun *Ecce Romani*, a Latin immersion program. MIT also requires SAT II test scores in math, science and either English or history. So, we are acquiring review guides for those tests, going through them to see if there is anything that still needs to be covered, and then he will take those tests. He is also beginning a Composition program, which simply means that David has to occasionally write descriptive paragraphs of short stories or other things he has read or essays about some a topic of his choice or mine. Also, he plans to take some science courses through the dual-enrollment program at the local community college over the next two school years. We decided to concentrate on the science courses at the college level because the lab work will be more difficult to accomplish at home. The community college classes will also begin to give him a taste of deadlines and more written work.

There were many reasons David chose MIT as *the* college he wished to attend, one being their atmosphere of cooperation and non-competitiveness. Another reason was that their undergraduates are encouraged and allowed to work hands-on with some of the most cutting edge technology and experiments. With this in mind, and knowing that MIT only accepts one in every eleven applicants, I am also looking at other colleges, hoping to find a few that he might also wish to apply to. One book I have found to be particularly informative is *Colleges That Change Lives*, by Loren Pope. Pope explores forty small, lesser-known colleges that offer diverse programs, small classes with more interaction between the students and faculty, and collaborative rather than competitive programs. I am hopeful we will find a couple of possibilities to explore more fully.

Motivation

I hear from many homeschooling parents who are worried about their teen's apparent lack of motivation. I sympathize, since that is a worry my husband and I have with David. Even though it is his desire to attend MIT and he knows what he must do to accomplish this, he is easily distracted and lacks motivation to do it on his own. He would much rather work on his computer games or read the latest fantasy book than pick up the math book or remember to review for the SAT. He asks me to remind him to do so, and so I do, and sometimes that simple reminder is enough to get him focused on his goals for the day. But it is a fine line between reminding and nagging. At times I have to just sit back and tell myself that he will not learn to manage his own time wisely if he doesn't suffer some consequences and that only he can truly motivate himself. I realize the consequences might be high, but at this point they won't be life threatening. Now is the time for him to understand that a dream does not become reality without effort, without the motivation and determination to make it come true. What's the worst case scenario? David might discover that he has to work an extra year to prepare for admission to that school of his dreams because he did not stick to the needed schedule. Or he may find that he ends up at another school for undergraduate work and then applies to MIT for graduate work. Whatever the consequences, ultimately it is up to David to find his own motivation.

At fourteen, our youngest child, Charles, does not lack for motivation and already he is on a very different path than either of his siblings. Charles is a late learning reader, still working to master the written word, so homeschooling has been a blessing for him. He has been able to work at his own pace, relying upon my reading aloud to him, along with videos, software, audio books, and hands-on learning for much of his educational experience.

Over the years it has been obvious that Charles will never be happy at any career which does not involve a lot of physical activity. He has a very high energy level and he seems most willing and able to tackle academic subjects on those days when he has been the most physically active. Some of the possible careers that he has mentioned over the years included dairy farmer (while we were living on our farm), NBA player (during his basketball-obsessing years), U. S. Park Ranger, zookeeper, falconer (one who trains falcons, hawks, etc.), landscaper, basketball coach, movie stunt man, and martial arts instructor. The last one, martial arts instructor, has been at the forefront since he began taking karate lessons. He has developed a passion for almost everything concerning the martial arts and is fairly certain (as certain as a fourteen-year-old can be) that the martial arts will be a major focus of his adult life, including his career. He takes lessons at a wonderful karate school and will have his black belt in another few months. The owners of the karate school (a homeschool family) are aware of Charles' interest in being an instructor and possibly one day owning his own karate school, so they are doing all they can to help him towards that goal. He has been learning how to instruct others, how to encourage students in their efforts while correcting their moves or positions, and how to deal with students that perhaps are not working up to their potential. He volunteers to assist with classes and other karate events (tournaments, birthday parties, etc.) as frequently as possible (which is pretty much as often as I'll agree to drive him there!). And occasionally the instructor has asked Charles to do some one-on-one instruction with lower-ranked students. All of this has given Charles a taste for what it would be like to be an instructor and he has discovered that not only does he really enjoy it, but also he seems to be good at it.

Charles is very sure he does not want to spend four years getting a college degree in anything, unless it were the martial arts! Instead, his goal right now is to someday own his own karate school, so he is very interested in pursuing what he would need to know to operate such a business. He talks of taking business courses at the local community college when he is old enough to participate in the dual-enrollment program. He wants to learn about accounting, finance, banking, and business procedures—anything and everything that might be helpful in owning and operating a business. Here again, his karate instructor is proving to be an invaluable resource. In addition to hiring Charles as an instructor when he has his black belt, he will also have the opportunity to learn the business end of operating a dojo (karate school),. And in another year or so, whenever Charles feels he is ready, he has been offered the opportunity to go for more training to another karate school where his instructor has sent his own daughter for training in operating a dojo.

In addition to karate, Charles has other subjects he wished to learn more about, such as first aid (he would like to take a Red Cross First Aid Course), how the human body works, eastern medicine and religions, and anything that is any way connected with martial arts. And lest one think he has no other interests, he also likes history, military campaigns, animals, and computer games, although he has no interest in creating them like his brother does, but simply in playing them.

Trust and Unschooling Go Hand In Hand

As you can see, it is possible to unschool through the high school years, to allow your children the freedom to follow their interest. It takes creativity and effort from both parent and child in locating resources and opportunities and thinking outside of the box. Unschooling through high school also requires faith in your children and their abilities and a strong measure of patience. I have discovered that it helps to take up a hobby so you do not spend too many of your waking hours obsessing about the future of your children!

And yes, your children will one day become motivated, although likely it will not happen according to your timetable. We would all love to see motivated fourteen-year-olds, thinking and planning for their future. But the reality is that many children are not ready to do this and may not be until they are sixteen or seventeen. Some may even need an extra year of "high school" to reach the point where they are ready to tackle college or life on their own. Also keep in mind the distinct possibility that, when your children do become motivated, that motivation may very well send them in a direction that you had not considered and that you definitely would not have planned for them. That is where trust comes in! You will have raised your children to think for themselves and in order to do so, they will need to follow where their heart and head leads them. Ultimately, it's their life, their dreams, and their goals. It's our job to insure a love of learning, the ability to learn, and the confidence that they can learn, along with our love and acceptance. The rest is up to them!

Time Management

How will Homeschooled children learn time management if they do not adhere to a schedule similar to that of public school? Will they be able to hold down a job or run their own business if they don't learn time management skills? These are questions that are often asked of certain homeschoolers, especially unschoolers and relaxed homeschoolers. I know this is an area that has concerned my husband during our unschooling journey.

Why do people believe that the public school system teaches time management? Is it because students are required to arise at a certain time each day, attend classes at certain hours each day, and must perforce, be in bed at a particular time each time in order to repeat the whole routine another day? Does that teach time management? Or does that just become a routine, an automatic movement through each day without really thinking? Are the students really learning to control their own time, or is their time being controlled by outside forces?

Those worried about time management believe that one lacks a specific schedule, set out in advance, that means one have no schedule at all and thus practices no time management skills. In our family's case, this is simply not true. Our daily schedule is set by the activities we are involved in on that day, and we modify our time management to suit that specific day. On days where we will be away from home due to activities, we will need to adjust the day before and/or the day afterwards to accommodate those things (both school and life related) that we must accomplish at home. Our schedule and time management changes on a daily basis, as needed.

I also do not believe you can "teach" someone time management, and most certainly not by adhering to some artificially imposed schedule. You may be able to assist someone who wishes to follow a particular schedule by gentle reminders or setting timer, etc., but the motivation for the time management must come from within the individual else any and all assistance will be for naught.

In our family, I have noticed each individual has their own inner time sense. For some, this inner sense is much stronger than for others, enabling them to keep track of the passage of time more easily and to better gauge the amount of time a certain task will take. Those with a strong inner time sense are more naturally "schedule" type personalities, setting and following their own internal schedules far better than any schedule I could impose. And those without the strong inner time sense find it difficult to adhere to any outside imposed schedule, and even, to some degree, their own internally imposed schedule, if they so desire to set one.

I am not a schedule type personality, but over the years of running a family and having to get people to places at certain times, I have learned to estimate how much I can accomplish in a set amount of time. It's been a long process.....and inevitably we are still either several minutes early (the first to arrive) or several minutes late; rarely do we make it to an event or activity exactly on time. I am a product of public schools; yet the outside imposed scheduling did nothing to help my internal time sense.

My husband complains about co-workers that punch in at 8am, and then go get their coffee, check their e-mail, make phone calls home, and finally, maybe, really begin to be productive at 8:20 or so. These co-workers are all products of the public school system, yet they did not learn how to manage their time wisely. Of course, this could also be tied into how strong their work ethic is, but I believe it also indicates that they did not learn to manage their time wisely.

Our youngest child has always had a finely tuned sense of the passage of time and how he needs to use his time. He knows, from the second he arises, just what he has to get done each day and the time frame he has. He knows which karate class(es) he wants to attend, what objectives he has for the day, and most of the time accomplishes them with little or no assistance from me (assistance in the form of reminders). His finely tuned inner time sense can be very annoying to the rest of us, though. For example, when he was younger, on errand-running days he would want to know in advance every place we were going and the order in which we were going to them. If the order deviated in any way, if we missed a stop or added a stop, he was vocally very unhappy. He would loudly demand why the changes, almost to the point of tears, because he had planned his thinking around the order of the stops we were going to make. Even now, at thirteen, if his daily schedule gets changed in any way, he can be out of sorts for several minutes afterwards, although he has learned not to express his displeasure and confusion in quite such negative ways.

Our middle child (15) is the most like me when it comes to time management and an inner time sense. He loses track of time very easily and then feels badly that he didn't accomplish what he really wanted to for that day. He needs timers set or repeated reminders that he wanted to accomplish this or that, especially if it is accomplishing something he knows he needs to do, but not necessarily something he enjoys doing. But, if it is robotics club day or something that he wants to do, really want to do, he will be more motivated and manage his time more wisely. That's not to say he doesn't still get absorbed by the computer or Legos and lose track of time, needing some gentle reminders from me, but he does do better. And, over the years I have seen an improvement in this as we have let him manage his own time as much as possible. He has suffered the consequences of being late or not getting something done he wanted to do and so is slowly developing his own time management skills through experience.

In the past, my husband has expressed worry about our children's late sleeping habits. He wondered whether they would be able to work a regular job and what would happen if they had to work a morning shift? Not everyone can work the late night shift, he would say! Well, he can now look at our eldest child and realize that, when the motivation is there, time management can follow. A year ago our eldest (now 18) was sleeping until 2pm, spending long hours on the computer and doing her school work in the wee hours of the morning. A year later she has a job which entails opening the store at 4am almost every day. She has been doing that for over two months now with no missed work. In addition, she's taking college classes, rarely on the computer at all, and working other shifts at the store (sometimes closing back to back with opening). Clearly, when the need was there, she was able to manage her time just fine.

Allowing children to experience the results of poor time management allows them the opportunities to develop the time management skills that will mesh well with their own inner time sense (and this can take several years). Obviously it would seems easier for parents to step in and impose what they think their child needs to do, but in the long run, this may not be best for the child. We must also realize that not all individuals are going to develop or practice good time management skills; some individuals may find this so contrary to their own inner time sense and their own personalities that they are just not able to do so.

Karen M. Gibson lives and learns with her family in Alabama, where they have experienced the freedom of home education since 1996. She is a freelance writer with her own website http://LeapingFromTheBox.com.

Top 20 Reasons to Homeschool Your Children

20. Your children never tell you you're a lot dumber that their teacher.

19. If you can't find matching socks for your children first thing in the morning. Who cares?

18. Cleaning out the refrigerator can double as chemistry lab.

17. Your children have good reason to think they might get punished in school, but no reason to think   they'll get beat up by a gang.

16. If the principal gives the teacher a bad evaluation, she can stick her icy feet against his legs at night.

15. You can post the Ten Commandments on your school room wall and won't get sued.

14. You never have to drive your child's forgotten lunch to school.

13. Your child will never go to their 20th high school reunion, meet an old flame and recklessly abandon their marriage.

12. You get to change more than diapers; you get to change their minds.

11. If you get caught talking to yourself, you can claim you're having a PTA meeting.

10. It's better to be slightly concerned about socialization than very concerned about socialism.

9. Your child will never suffer the embarrassment of group showers after PE.

8. The only debate about the school lunch program is whose turn it is to cook.

7. You never have to face the dilemma of whether to take your child's side or the teacher's side in a dispute at school.

6. If your child gets drugs at school, it's probably Tylenol.

5. The teacher gets to kiss the principal in the faculty lounge and no one gossips.

4. Your kids recognize that this list is numerically in reverse order.

3. Your honor student can actually read the bumper sticker that you have on your car.

2. If your child claims that the dog ate his homework, you can ask the dog.

1. Some day your children will consider you to be a miracle working expert and will turn to you for advice.

Author Unknown

Chapter Seven
Pearls of Wisdom:

Baldwin County Homeschoolers

This article was originally published in the Baldwin County Home Educators Association Newsletter: Home's Cool Herald.

The Journey of Homeschooling

Please us your imagination to help me paint a picture. Feet firmly planted on the solid deck of the sailing schooner fast underway, you look out across the expansive blue water, straining to see what is really not possible to envision……the future.

Only a short time ago, you cast off from a comfortable secure place, turning your back on the familiar past and facing the future with great excitement and anticipation. Only now, as you gaze out ahead, unable to focus on any tangible destination, you experience a little nagging feeling deep down. Perhaps this voyage was a little hasty, premature. Perhaps, you should have trained for it a little longer…. Say ten years or more would do.

But the wind in your face mixed with the mist of the colliding waves once again stirs up that sense of mystery and mission which intrigued you from the beginning of this journey. Doubt and hope. One on each side of the coin. Which will it be?

You lift your eyes upward as if looking for the answer. There, shining brilliantly and steadily through the grayness of the upcoming night, that star-spectacular point of light reminds you of His truth, His faithfulness, His word. Then, you remember Him.

Turning, you barely discern in the darkness, the comforting, strong form silently standing guard at the helm of this huge vessel. Although you cannot see, His very presence is more than sufficient in dashing all your fears away.

With a long sigh, you look out ahead once more, and you stand just a little taller. The wind rushes into your face, and you feel the tingle of knowing that you are on a great and marvelous adventure. You're off on the journey of homeschooling.

Bon Voyage and God Bless,

Trinka Brabston

Tips from Homeschool Mothers

These next few pages are comments from homeschool mothers who talk about their best tips for successful homeschooling taken from the Baldwin County Home Educators Association official newsletter: Home's Cool Herald.

Sally Deane:

I guess my best advice would be not to "sweat" the small stuff. The goal is to teach the child to be self-motivated, creative, and most importantly, how to think. Pay attention and pick up on things that the child is interested in; use those things to motivate him to read, write, etc. Sometimes your teaching methods may seem unconventional, but follow your "gut" feelings and let the Lord lead you in learning experiences that will foster the child's imagination, creativity and will challenge him to think.

Robin Hutchinson:

Where is your child spending most of his/her time? Remember....Fathers train up your child in the way he should go and when he is old he will not depart from it. Families who have so many irons in the fire can sometimes cause the parents to feel like they are running a hotel instead of a home. I've been guilty of this and heard a wonderful message on slowing down and giving your children down time at home. It's important to make them accountable to the family and so on.

Lisa Johnson

I would advise all homeschoolers, especially those new to homeschooling, to try to find a support group and participate in it. I don't think it is wise to try to do this tremendously important job "in a vacuum". We can always benefit from the experiences of those who have done this longer, and we need to have friends we can talk with a pray with who understand what we are going through. My very spiritual answer is that we need to remember to go to the Lord with every issue concerning this honor He has called us to, because if He has called us to do this, He will provide what we need for every circumstance. He's a very good administrator.

Teaching my children from the Christian curriculums we're using is giving me the Christian education I did not get when I was growing up. I went to public schools and remember being so confused in science class about how my beliefs as a Christian could fit in with all the "facts" we were being taught in science, and I remember some of the literature we had to read was not very uplifting. I realized what a fantastic blessing I've been given being called to teach my children things I didn't get the first time around. What a joy it is to still be learning!

Felicia Coker:

I assure all the moms this one tip will make each and every day a success. Get up an hour or two ahead of your children. On the mornings that I get up I….

prepare a fresh fruit salad for an early breakfast

make rice, start a roast, or any other thing to get a head start on lunch or dinner.

start a load of clothes in the washer

make sure the day's lesson plans are complete

and make myself a cup of yerba' mate and talk to God.

This never fails. We have a wonderfully organized day full of good attitudes. Good or bad, your attitude is contagious.

Bebe Ross:

I was fortunate enough to get to spend some time one with another homeschool mother/friend under a beautiful, old oak tree at Beckwith Lodge following a ladies' Bible study/ retreat. In her calm and serene tone she told me that she and he husband believed that establishing a "family home school mission statement" was the most critical step in success. She assured me that taking the time to pray over, think through and discuss this important aspect of your purpose and goals for your homeschool would be the most valuable time spent in preparation for the year and for your family. She encouraged me to actually put pen to paper and not just "have it in your head". That advice has helped me weather some big storms. I keep a copy of our mission statement in my lesson plan book. It is amazing how the Lord has uses that piece of paper to remind me of our purpose. She also shared that the most important teaching we do for our children is character training. Everything else is just icing on the cake.

Kally Wyatt:

I have given quite a bit of thought to homeschooling tips and what keeps coming to my mind is this: "Thank God everyday for the blessing of your children and the opportunity to teach and train them for life." If we look at homeschooling our children as a blessing, we will have more energy to accomplish this very important task. Secondly, "Whatever you do, work at it with all your heart as working for the Lord." (Colossians 3:23) We must keep in mind that training our children is one of the most important things we can do for the Lord. He has entrusted us with souls, let's count it joy to train them to love and obey our loving God. Let us count it joy to train them to work hard, study hard, become efficient in whatever they do and in so doing: honor God.

Sarah Hofferber:

Pray first. You cannot do this alone! "Seek ye first the kingdom of God". (Matthew 6:33-34) When I become overwhelmed, frustrated, or unsure of what to do regarding school, I find it is time to stop and ask, "Have you prayed about this today?"

If you have more than one child, do subjects together whenever possible. Some subjects are more conducive to this, such as Art, Music, History, Bible, Literature or Science. Even if your children are 2 or 3 grades apart, you can use the grade level in between or the oldest grade level with modifications.

Do not be a slave to your curriculum. Make it serve you instead.

Establish a regular reading time for your child every day. Even if it is for 30 minutes at night before bed or during afternoon quiet time, this is an excellent habit. It works whether you read aloud to them or they read independently.

I purchased an inexpensive 5x7 commercial type rug (no pile) for Lego's cars or other small items. My toddler/small children had to keep all pieces on this rug. If I found these items off of the rug, they were put away for a certain length of time. The rug was placed near our school table and was a very helpful to control messes. Also, we bought different colors of narrow removable art tape to make roads, runways, buildings, animal pastures, etc. This encouraged imagination and was easy to cleanup. One other positive outcome was that very young children can learn so much from the older children's school time while they are "just playing" nearby.

When we read our Bible chapter in the morning, I had my children draw a picture of what we were reading about. They had to pay attention to know what to draw, and I have some adorable pictures that are some of my favorite, such as the Tower of Babel and their idea of what God looks like.

We have found it helpful to take a quick cleanup break (5-15 minutes) around mid-morning when everyone starts to get restless. We all pitch in to start laundry, put away papers, make notes in journal/planner, straighten up, etc. Also pick up at the end of school day and in the evening after supper.

To me the worst thing seems to be for a school
principally to work with methods
of fear, force, and artificial authority.
Such treatment destroys the sound
sentiments, the sincerity, and
the self-confidence of the pupil.
It produces the submissive subject.

--Albert Einstein

Chapter Eight
Homeschooling the Hard-To-Teach

By
Debbie Hanson

Picture a mother in a chair, surrounded by her loving children. One child is cuddling in her lap. Two are at her feet. All are reading serenely by the crackling fire.

If this phenomenon has never occurred in your home, you're not alone.

If the picture were taken at my house, the boy would be on the couch with his feet in the air. The book would be upside down on the floor, totally forgotten. Then the boy would be busy wrestling the dog, inventing weapons or taking apart something. Better yet, he'd be throwing things in the fire that didn't belong there.

Welcome to the world of the Hard-to-Teach child.

As I write this, I've had conversations with at least four homeschooling moms who are discouraged, frustrated and feeling like they're terrible teachers. I'm one of them. We feel like we're getting nowhere and accomplishing nothing.

Not coincidentally, each of us has at least one child I call Hard-to-Teach.

What is a Hard-To-Teach child?

It's hard to define, because each child is different. I can tell you these are usually *not* the children winning national spelling bees, reading classic books for fun, studying Latin at age 6 or entering college at age 12. Homeschooling is becoming famous for producing such prodigies. I can almost guarantee none of the children exhibiting such behavior were in the Hard-to-Teach category.

While their cohorts are studying Biblical Greek, the Hard-to-Teach children are hanging from trees (or chandeliers). Their mothers are bodily dragging them before the books, pencils and paper that constitute requirements of learning. The children longingly look out the windows while the moms are considering long-term therapy.

Hard-to-Teach children often have the attention span of a mosquito and sit still just as often. They like to take apart toys to see how they work – especially the expensive, electronic type. Of course, because of the fore-mentioned attention span problem, they can't remember how to put those toys back together.

Reading is boring or a painful chore, math is a confusion of useless numbers, and handwriting is something only the kid or his loving mother can read – and often they don't have a clue what's on the paper.

Some of these kids add to the fun by reversing their letters and numbers, even in the sixth and seventh grades.

Welcome to my world.

My son is a loving, giving young man. He can shoot a ball at any hoop, hit any target with his BB gun, and fix things I can't. He will work like a man at age 12. But put a pencil in his hand, and that's when the trouble starts. The most seasoned State Department bureaucrats should study my son's skills at delay tactics once we sit down for school.

If you can relate to this kind of child, you probably have what the experts call a kinesthetic learner – a child who learns by doing. They are Hard-to-Teach, because the usual methods don't work very well.

Parents whose Hard-to-Teach children are ensconced in a classroom usually say, "I could never homeschool James. He'd drive me crazy."

To whom I answer, "Yes, you can. In fact, these are the kids who particularly need homeschooling."

A kinesthetic learner has no place in a classroom, particularly when they are young, because classroom methods rarely work well for them. They need to handle and experience things, not watch them, hear them or read them. A teacher with 20-30 children to patrol can't possibly let all of them experience and handle everything, so kinesthetic learning techniques just aren't practical for her. Out come the books and paper.

It's my inexpert opinion that many of the children "diagnosed" as ADD or ADHD are kinesthetic learners who weren't hard-wired to sit still all day. In the old days on the farm or in the blacksmith shop, that was a good thing. Our industrialized society now wants its active young people to harness that energy and channel it into a moving pencil.

We need to quit assuming there is something wrong with our energy-enhanced children. What *is* erroneous is our cookie-cutter expectation of how he or she ought to learn. The usual methods don't work. Rather than label our kids (which I've been guilty of doing, too), we need to find new methods.

The good news is these children are often bright. When they're enjoying something, attention spans expand exponentially and they will remember the fine points of what is being taught. The hard part is finding the keys to their brains.

I don't claim to know even half of what I should, but here are some suggestions for those who are considering homeschooling a Hard-to-Teach child, or are currently struggling with teaching one or more of them.

ADJUST THE FOCUS

What's Important? - Early in our homeschooling journey, my husband and I decided the most important thing for our son to learn was that God is real, and He works in our lives. We agreed if we could "raise up a child in the way he should go" spiritually, then we had done a good job. When I get most frustrated, I try and return to that foundation. Though my son can't spell some tremendously easy words, at 12 he's told us twice he wants to be a minister, and once that he wants to be a missionary. I'm realistic enough to know those plans may change 100 times before he is grown, but if he becomes a ditch digger or a rocket designer, I'm encouraged that his heart is focused on the Lord.

Celebrate The Strengths – If your child is good at fixing things, cooking, athletics, music or any other pursuit, tell her so! Be glad someone else will change the light bulbs and fix the leaky faucets.

Our Hard-to-Teach son was 11 when we built our house. We had a contractor finish the sheet rock, and then we did all our own interior flooring and painting. Our son learned to cut correct lengths of tongue-in-groove boards for our wood floors, nailed in all the sub-flooring for the tile floors, and helped build a drainage system to redirect the water which would race down our sloping lawn. He shoveled red clay and helped spread 22 tons of rock for our driveway, wheelbarrow load by wheelbarrow load. We couldn't have done it all without him.

Just today he fixed a space heater that I thought was broken because it wouldn't come on. "Aw, Mom," he said. "You just have the thermostat set wrong."

He hauls our firewood, feeds our menagerie of animals, and is a tremendous help inside and outside the house, (when forced.) His greatest thrill is to see me ineptly attempting to do something with a hammer or pliers. "Let me do that for you, Mom," he says with his best masculine swagger.

After all, why is it preferable to excel in scholarly pursuits than in crafts or trades? Only because our society says so. Interestingly, that is a humanist Greek idea. Our spiritual forefathers, the Hebrews, expected everyone to work hard with their bodies.

As Paul, a theologian AND tentmaker, wrote: **"Make it your ambition to lead a quiet life, to mind your own business and to *work with your hands,* just as we told you, so that your daily life may win the respect of outsiders and so that *you will not be dependent on anybody." (1 Thess. 4:11, NIV. Emphasis mine.)*

If working with your hands is good enough for Paul, why not for us? Think about it: who makes more money: a professional football player or a rocket scientist? How many academicians are in need of a decent-paying job? Plenty. How many expert and reliable plumbers can't find work? I don't know a one.

Trades and crafts are necessary and valuable. As our society becomes increasingly technical, the need for people who know how to fix all these machines will continue to grow.

Amusingly, just the other day our son was sitting in our completed living room. He looked around and said, "You ... it was more fun building this house than living in it."

Viva la difference!

But, much as we appreciate our children's accomplishments outside classroom, in order to ensure their well-rounded, proper development not to mention comply with the law – we must educate them. This is where the fun begins.

METHODS THAT DON'T WORK

I'll start here, because I've tried them.

◆   Reading glowing accounts of how much homeschooled children are ahead of their peers is depressing for the parents of the Hard-to-Teach. The best use for such reports is starting fires.

◆   Screaming, threatening and extra school workloads are a waste of time. You both end up miserable.

◆   Comparing the child to his more serene and accomplished sibling or cousin is useless, and just ends up in resentment.

◆   Beating your head against the desk doesn't work either. It gives you a headache, and lets the little sucker know you've lost control.

Setting the child free to do what he or she wants to do is mpting, and is occasionally a last resort when everyone is worn out. However, it doesn't teach them to read or do multiplication tables.

METHODS THAT WORK

Expect Delayed Development – Often kinesthetic learners will be the first ones to ride their bikes and the last ones to begin reading. Not all children begin riding a bike by age 5, and no one calls them stupid. But if a child isn't ready to read by age 6 -- the "standard" age for first grade- he or she is considered dumb. Give the kinesthetic child time to develop. If they are begging to read and studying on their own, great. Get them started. If they are not, work on identifying letters and numbers; then learn by doing. They will catch up, I promise – but not if they've learned to hate school before they hardly get started.

Read Aloud – One way to make school more appealing is to read aloud to your children. They will learn to enjoy the sound of the written language, develop a larger vocabulary, and often retain much more than you realize. When he was younger, my son used to roll around on the floor while I was reading to him. It drove me crazy, but when I asked him what I had read, he could repeat it almost verbatim. Don't just read fiction, either. These kids like how-to books, biographies and little-known facts.

When you're tired of reading, check out excellent books on tape from your local library. Be sure to get ones above your child's reading level.

They will listen to them over and over again, acquiring a taste for exceptional vocabulary and superb prose.

Phonics –Hooked on Phonics really does work. It has cards to turn for the visual and kinesthetic effect. I gave my son a pair of his own headphones for the tapes, which appeal to the auditory side. We used the book for reinforcement. He basically taught himself, which was a wonderful break for me. It was so effective that at age 12, I'm considering going back for a refresher course because of my son's spelling challenges. The cost is prohibitive, so you might want to try creating your own phonics program using tapes and cards. I don't suggest just a book approach. Our busy children need more stimulation than words that just lay there on a page.

Visualization – For a child to remember something, it helps tremendously for them to visualize what they have learned. Drawing or creating is a wonderful way to do this. I have my son draw pictures of what he has read in the Bible to cement the story in his mind. He remembers the concept, and I have some wonderful pictures of Moses and the gate to heaven, among others. For this reason, the Hard-To-Teach child often loves science, which is hands-on. Don't just read about science, do the experiments, take the walks, make the leaf collections. They love it, and they'll remember every bit of it for years.

Frequent Breaks - Kinesthetic learners require frequent breaks from concentrated learning. During these breaks, make sure the kids do something physical. Chores are always a good choice. On our first break, we often go make our beds or wash breakfast dishes. The second break, I send him outside.

Timers – We use the kitchen stove timer for two reasons. The first is to make sure he doesn't work too long sitting still, because then we waste time. That sounds like a contradiction, but it's not. For about 20 minutes, my son will work very hard. Then he "zones out," and he fiddles with his pencil and paper, or writes nonsense. Or stares. After 20 minutes, he gets a 5 or 10 minute break, then goes back to school. During that break, we do something physical, as mentioned before. The timer is set again, so I remember to call him back from whatever he's doing. Trust me – he's not coming back on his own!

Incidentally, we use the kitchen timer, which is in another room, because a timer in the schoolroom where we work is distracting. He hears the tick-tick-tick, or sees the seconds passing. There goes the concentration.

Give Them Something to Beat Up – For whatever reason, kinesthetic learners think better when moving. When my son has to concentrate, I give him something quiet to put in his hands. It might be a small stuffed animal, a gel-filled beanbag, or even just a rag. While he's thinking of answers, he'll throw the object from hand to hand, squish it, or beat it within an inch of its life . . . but he'll come up with the right answer.

Use the Computer - What a great innovation! There are tons of educational games that will stimulate learning and reinforce concepts. If you don't have one, make trips to the library part of your curriculum. Most of them have games for children. I use computer games as a reward for good work, or a "substitute" when I'm not feeling well.

If you teach your child to type using one of the many programs out there, he or she can use the wonder of Spell check as well!

Lower Distractions – Bright colors on the walls, Mozart playing on the stereo, and the dog warming your feet sounds like a picture-perfect learning environment – unless you have an easily distractible child. The quieter and less distracting, the better. Shut the door. Close the curtains. Have as few sounds as possible. If your space is limited, set their desk in a corner with nothing on the walls, or clear out a closet and put the desk in there, especially if you have younger children running around. Anything we can do to help them focus makes a difference. My son has even complained that the kitchen-type clock on the wall irritates him because he can hear the very quiet ticking.

Field Trips and Multi-Media – A single trip is worth a week of explaining, but use both to drive home learning. For example, you might read about Martin Luther King to celebrate his birthday in January. Then you may want to watch a video of his speeches. At this point you might want to plan a trip to a Civil Rights memorial. For those who live in the Southeast, it could be interesting to drive the road from Selma to Montgomery, Ala., or visit the area in Memphis where MLK met his fatal bullet. Mid-Westerners might visit the tenement where he lived in Chicago. What fun is it to homeschool if we can't go see things?

Points / Rewards – We set up a system of points which are worth privileges, new pencils, small toys, or breaks. For work accomplished correctly, he gets a certain number of points. For poor performance, bad attitude, or interrupting, points are taken away. This is a very effective strategy – when I remember to use it. Which brings me to my next method.

Structure – This, I confess, is my biggest challenge. On the one hand, I have to be flexible and innovative enough to figure out ways for my son to learn and remember things. On the other, I need to create an environment that is structured to make the learning environment friendly to the easily distracted. I am a free-form person who feels suffocated by too much structure, so it's a frustrating fine line for both of us.

I have found, however, that when I am most irritated by his lack of learning, I discover that my structure has dissolved into chaos. At that point, we have to realign and get back on track.

Lower the Volume of Work - It's important to have a regular time to start school, or otherwise you'll find it's 1 p.m. and no school has happened. On the other hand, with younger Hard-to-Teach children, you can only expect to get 2-3 hours of good study out of them before they're on overload. I've learned to lower the volume of work without lowering the difficulty. For example, a math book that has lessons with 25 daily problems has proven to be too much. We will do 6 – 7 problems. If he gets those, then he's done for the day. If he doesn't, then we do a few more until he gets it.

We've learned to do 10 spelling words a week, instead of 20. We write one-page reports, instead of three. We will read aloud together, as well as allowing him to read silently. The learning is still going on, but in manageable bites. Too much work becomes overwhelming for these children and he or she will shut down.

Find Something in Which They Excel – All children need more than book learning, but particularly kids who are having a hard time in school. Find what your child excels in. It may be a challenge. Perhaps it's athletics, dance, music, theater, or sewing. Maybe it's cooking or sailing. One child who is struggling with reading at age ten is one of the best in his homeschool Spanish language class.

Keep trying things until you find what clicks with your child. When children have areas in which they are accomplished, it builds confidence and improves attitudes. Lessons can be expensive, but look for ones sponsored by city programs, or barter. Perhaps you are good at writing, and your friend teaches piano. Offer to trade teaching. Maybe you can exchange home-grown produce for fencing lessons. Our homeschool organization arranges classes and schedules gym times during early afternoons when other children are in school. Consequently, we often get major discounts.

Apprenticeships – As your children grow older, allow them to go to work -- for free or pay -- with people who work with their hands. Our energetic children usually love to work, and will work hard. Maybe they could learn to build and create with wood, repair the plumbing, or run a tractor. They might assist the local veterinarian, or learn to fix electrical appliances. For thousands of years, young people became apprentices to learn a working trade. Why have we stopped doing this?

One homeschooling friend allowed her son to spend his senior year working with a computer web site designer. It sparked an interest in the ever-burgeoning field of computers.

Apprenticeships are legitimate learning, and instill confidence in young people. While the child might not decide on the apprenticeship job for a career, he or she can acquire lifelong skills much more practical for most of us than learning calculus.

Debbie M. Hanson is a former award-winning journalist. She taught herself to read at age 4, was reading classics in the second grade, and graduated in the top five percent of her college class. She's been home educating her Hard-to-Teach child for four years, and is still somewhat mystified as to why God would find it amusing to present her with such a challenge. She has never used world geography, chemistry, or algebra for any purpose in her adult life. Her son is much smarter at figuring out what's wrong with things than she is. She is married to another writer who can't fix anything either. They are praying their son grows up to be an auto mechanic or something else equally useful.

There is a time in every man's education
when he arrives at the conviction that
envy is ignorance;
that imitation is suicide;
that he must take himself for better, for worse,
as his portion;
that through the wide universe is full of good,
no kernel of nourishing corn can come to him
but through his toil bestowed on that plot of ground
which is given to him to till.

--Ralph Waldo Emerson

Chapter Nine
Keeping Close To The Vine

By
Lisa Hyman Johnson

My husband and I were watching the three-year-olds play in the nursery during the church service when one of our friends started talking about how she homeschooled her children.

"You're a teacher, aren't you?" my friend asked me. "You really ought to consider homeschooling Leah when she's older."

Home what? I had to admit that I didn't even know what my friend was talking about, and besides, Eric and I had everything all planned. I would try to get a teaching job at the Christian school supported by our church in a couple of years when Leah started kindergarten so I could still sort of be close to her. Maybe later when she was older I could leave teaching and work full-time as a children's writer, a dream I'd had for a long time. But when Anita explained what homeschooling was and that it was legal, I couldn't stop thinking about it. Could I teach our little girl? Should I? Did God have another plan in mind for us?

After thinking and praying about it constantly, Eric said to me one day, "I can't think of a better teacher for Leah than you." We began to believe that God was leading us to teach our children at home. We went from being parents who had never heard of homeschooling to advocates of a way of life that is as rewarding as it is challenging.

We first heard about homeschooling when Leah was just three, so there was no need to rush out to buy school books. I found as we built our home that Leah practiced counting bricks and could write her letters on the soon-to-be-covered floorboards. By the time she was four-and-a-half, we were moved in, had another child on the way, and Leah was making good progress with her three R's. Since I didn't have to leave Leah at school all day, she got to go with me to hear her unborn brother's heartbeat and help me with our pets when we took them in for checkups. But as she grew older, a little speech problem began to grow into a stumbling block for her. Leah stuttered so terribly that it took tremendous patience to listen to her tell anything. I knew that it would only get worse, but because we were not part of the school system, I didn't know how to find therapy for her that wouldn't cost a fortune. God led us to a lovely lady who worked with patients at our area hospital. She helped us find a way for insurance to cover some of therapy expenses, and soon learning "turtle talk" and other such games became part of our daily lessons. By the time she "graduated" from her sessions with "Mrs. Shelley," baby David (who would later need his own lessons in pronouncing "lizard L's" "and rooster R's") was starting to toddle around the hospital halls. It had been an investment of time and money, but Leah spoke so clearly and understandably that she has little recollection of ever having done anything differently. I believe that teaching her at home (following

Shelley's instructions), where her efforts were met with loving, patient instruction instead of ridicule from classmates helped her to overcome her stuttering with no trauma to her self-image. Because we had overcome that obstacle and because Leah learned so quickly, I thought that the biggest challenge I would have to face from then on would be handling a little one while teaching the older child. I soon learned that overcoming a speech problem would be small compared to the challenges yet to come.

In our earliest years of homeschooling, Leah was bright, artistic, and gifted with a very good memory. She could recite every book we read to her. Yet I began to notice when she began learning to read in the first grade that words Leah read easily on Monday were a mystery on Tuesday. Sometimes she misread a word she had read with no difficulty only moments before. She substituted words, swapped words, guessed words. Most of the time I was patient with her and I understood from my teaching days that it can take a while for students to remember new material, but I confess that there were also days when I accused her of not paying attention or goofing off. Some days she would cry, other days I cried, wondering if homeschooling had been a mistake. I begged God to show me what to do.

Then one Sunday Leah brought home a paper with her name neatly written backwards at the top. I thought of the other times when she had written words backwards and read them as if nothing were wrong. I remembered how my husband Eric could write and read backwards so well that often he had trouble reading correctly afterward. I also recalled him saying jokingly that he must be dyslexic because he had read something wrong on a sign at work or out driving. Suddenly, everything became clear. Eric was probably dyslexic, and his daughter was as well. I also realized that I was guilty of being impatient with her over something she could not help. I asked the Lord's forgiveness, as well as Leah's, and then prayed for direction on what to do next.

I wondered if the critics of homeschooling who claim that homeschooling parents are not trained to know how to handle educational problems might be right as I faced the daunting task of helping a child with learning difficulties. Then I realized that I was a trained educator with a master's degree, and nothing in my professional education had taught me how to handle any of the students I'd had with learning problems and that I'd done the best I could with each student with the resources I had at the time. I knew I had a lot more available for helping Leah, so, with the Lord guiding us, Eric and I began to find materials and methods for helping our daughter learn to read.

By the end of the third grade, Leah was reading nearly at grade level. Though she is now chronologically in the eighth grade, she is doing freshman-level work quite well and is a voracious reader. Her spelling still reveals her dyslexia, but her skills in art and music more than make up for misspelled words. Her brother is dyslexic as well, but because of what I learned in teaching Leah, David did not have to suffer through some of the same problems she and I had. Both of them are well aware of their dyslexia, but because they have not had to suffer the humiliation that students in schools often experience because of going to "special classes" and being "learning disabled," they accept themselves as God made them, knowing their strengths and weaknesses and having positive self-images. They have been able to learn with materials and at a pace that has been best for them form a teacher who knows them, loves them, and ahs all the time in the world to help them with whatever they need. In this area of our lives alone, homeschooling has been a blessing that I cannot praise enough. And yet another challenge loomed ahead for our family, one that would test our faith and make homeschooling not just an educational option but also a necessity.

Early in the year 2000, Leah began to mention that her joints felt stiff and painful. After many tests and many days of increasing pain, a pediatric rheumatologist confirmed what I had been suspecting. Leah had juvenile rheumatoid arthritis. Every joint was affected, as well as the connective tissue around her lungs. We had to be on guard for damage to her heart as well as her eyes. We were given the best medication available to children at that time and Leah began several types of therapy, but nothing relieved her excruciating pain. I shared our situation with our homeschool support group and asked them to pray for us. Our special group prayed and more. Calls and cards were frequent, as well as cookies and covered dishes. One thing that our homeschooling friends did that touched us deeply was when several families visited one day and gave Leah a large box. When she opened it, she was speechless with surprise. Our friends had all contributed money to buy her an American Girl doll. I think for that moment her pain was forgotten, and we will always remember what they did.

I do not know how families deal with such a situation when their chronically ill children attend school, but for us homeschooling was a blessing that God had provided for that difficult time in our lives. We had to arrange her schedule around sleepless nights, countless therapy sessions, and medication schedules, but she only missed two days of school because of doctor visits. Little David patiently learned to do his work independently while I spent extra time with his sister. Sometimes the work had to be done orally because holding the pencil was too painful for her, and studying math was especially difficult because the pain mad it hard to concentrate but with God's help we kept on as well as we could.

I cannot begin telling this story without sharing how it ended. Because none of the conventional or alternative medications and therapies helped to relieve Leah's suffering, we began to sense that God was leading us to take a step of faith and trust Him to heal her according to His Word in James 5:31: "Is any one of you sick? He should call the elders of the church to pray over him and anoint him with oil in the name of the Lord. And the prayer offered in faith will make the sick person well; the Lord will raise him up (NIV)." We asked our pastors and deacons to come to our home to pray for Leah's healing in this manner. We asked everyone who knew about her arthritis to be praying for her that night. Leah had such trust that Jesus was going to heal.

Lisa Hyman Johnson is the daughter of a Navy veteran and had lived all over the United States. She received her M.A. in English from Auburn University and taught high school English for several years. She is married to Eric Johnson and has a daughter, Leah, a son, David, and assorted cats and dogs. They live on the beautiful eastern shore of Mobile Bay in Daphne, Alabama, and attend Jubilee Baptist Church. Lisa has been writing since elementary school and has published a number of articles, poems, and short stories. In addition to teaching her children and writing, Lisa also serves as the Southwest Alabama/Southeast Mississippi regional coordinator for Operation Christmas Child, a project of Samaritan's Purse, an international relief ministry.

What does education often do? It makes a straight-cut ditch of a free, meandering brook.

--Henry David Thoreau

Chapter Ten
The Final Word

By
Valerie J. Steimle

From a recent "The Late, Late Show", Craig Kilborn jokingly made the comment from his "In the News" spot about homeschoolers:

"Parents having to get the socialization for their homeschooled children will make fun of their (children's) zits." Seen on CBS on January 30, 2004.

One of the biggest complaints from the rest of the world about homeschooling your children is that homeschool children do not get the "socialization" needed to be raised as a normal healthy person. There is a very good reason why this is false.

Children need the example of how a person should act from an adult. How is it that children can learn how to act civilly with each other when surrounded by children the same age as them all day? Children learn how to behave from parents and other adults. It's amazing how this works.

A very interesting report was done by Art Moore of the WorldNetDaily.com, posted October 23, 2003 called: "Homeschoolers New Political Force Refutes 'Socialization' Concerns Posed By Thinkers In Academia". Art Moore reported "an unprecedented new study of adults who were homeschooled not only contradicts assertions they lack socialization but shows them far more likely than the average American to be civilly minded and engaged in their local communities." Dr. Brian Ray of the National Home Education Research Institute in Salem, Oregon conducted a survey of 7,300 homeschooled adults and asked questions pertaining to their life as an adult after being homeschooled and found some interesting things. Dr. Ray explained that "people who doubt homeschoolers are becoming socialized typically have two presuppositions:

One is that for adequate ability in terms of social chit-chat and being able to talk at a cocktail party, you probably need to attend an institutional school for 13 years of your life, because that has been the norm for the last 100 years.

The second one is that schools run by state-certified teachers generally know the best ways for a child to acquire knowledge and world views."

He concluded that the first assumption has been found to be unwarranted by not only his study but several others on homeschooled children. No one needs 13 years of public school to know how to play and have a conversation with others.

The second assumption Dr. Ray says "is more difficult to deal with because it's more philosophical." What adults learn as children of a "world view largely depends on associations as people get older rather than the influence of the school system."

But then he did discover that homeschoolers are much more likely than others to align with the beliefs of their families. This survey showed homeschooled adults were responsible citizens, and believed strongly in the responsibility of parents raising their children. They were strong independent thinkers and for the most part participated in ongoing community service activities such as coaching a sports team, volunteering at a school or working with a church or neighborhood association. [5]

After having several conversations with other parents who look down on the homeschooling movement because of the socialization, I found this survey very refreshing and it squelched any doubts I had about homeschooled children the future of society. I knew my children were able to socialize with others without any problem and I knew other families who did the same thing didn't have a problem either.

Checklist

If you have decided to homeschool your child and are thinking about how to actually start, there is a great checklist of ideas on what to do before starting to homeschool from the magazine The Teaching Home dated March/April 1996 issue. You don't have to follow any other these or you can pick one out of the list but some of these ideas are very helpful. Check out their magazine for some good ideas on how to teach your children at home. (See Chapter 11)

1. Pray: Pray continually for wisdom, guidance and strength and make this a top priority.

2. Communication: Maintain good communication with your spouse at each step in the process of homeschooling. One parent may do most of the research, planning or teaching but the other should be informed and involved in decision-making and setting goals.

3. Goals: Write out or review your philosophy and long-range goals for your children's education and training.

4. Inventory: Take inventory of each child's knowledge, skills and character. You may use standardized tests, publisher's diagnostics or homemade oral or written examinations to accomplish this.

5. Objectives: Set objectives (another nice word for goals) for each child for this year that will move him or her toward your long-range goals. Several children in a family can share similar objectives in subjects like history and science. Discuss these objectives with each child privately and explain how they fit into the big picture of his/her future.

6. Methods: Consider various teaching methods, curriculum, and other available resources. Basic differences involve the degree of structure or flexibility you wish to use at each stage of your child's development. If possible, visit a curriculum fair.

7. Budget: Rework your budget, allocating funds for educational materials. You may be able to spend less on "school" clothes or transportation and emphasize learning tools, books, and games for gifts. Less expensive foods that require more preparation can cut costs and provide life skills education at the same time.

8. Reference Library: Add to your family's library of reference books, quality literature, and educational audiovisual aids, especially items that will help meet this year's objectives.

9. Libraries: Become familiar with your local library. Learn how to use its system for finding books by subject, title, or author and how to reserve books or order them through interlibrary loans. Explore the reference section. Also browse through your church library and see if Christian schools or Bible colleges will let you use their libraries.

10. Materials: Choose and list the methods and materials that you will use to meet your objectives for each child this year. Then, ideally, order or collect materials early. Textbooks or workbooks can be supplemented with unit studies with unit studies, games, projects etc., to cover all objectives.

11. Make plans to comply with your state laws as fully as possible and consider joining the Home School Legal Defense Association.

12. Household Organization: Do a thorough cleaning of your house. Get rid of unused items and store little-used ones out of the way. Designate a place for everything including space for books and school supplies.

13. Family Schedule: Reorganize your family's schedule and chore assignments to fit your educational activities. Train children to do household tasks and establish regular meal and bed times.

14. Discipline: Deal consistently with behavior or attitude problems.

15. Commitment: Be prepared to handle opposition or lack of immediate success through prayers, adjustment and perseverance.

16. Head Start: Establish nonacademic activities during the week to break up the monotony which might have registration deadlines several weeks before you start school.

17. Teacher Review: Study basic math and phonics skills and spelling rules yourself to prepare for presenting them to your children. Look through an English grammar handbook that you will use for reference. You can learn or review other material with your children later as they study it.

18. Calendar: Plan your year's calendar, marking school days, test days, holidays, vacations and special events.

19. Preparation: Familiarize yourself with your curriculum, noting unit divisions, and collect any needed supplementary materials.

20. Planning: Decide and list which topics, units or subjects you will cover during which weeks or months to make an overall plan for the year. Units can be shifted to coincide with related events or seasons.

21. School Schedule: Use your overall plan to develop your daily and weekly school schedule.

22. Celebrations: Plan special celebrations for the first day of school and for the completion of the first week or unit of study as well as the mastery of significant skills.

23. Explanations: Carefully explain your expectations and procedures to your children.

Beginning: Get started and keep going.

THIS IS IMPORTANT: Make changes and adjustments as needed.

This list is not to overwhelm you. This list is a guide for those parents totally lost or in need of some place to start. I think if I did every single thing on this check list I would be tearing my hair out. But know that preparation does take time and the more you prepare, the better you will feel when you start schooling your own children.

According to census officials, the number of homeschoolers in the United States is as high as 2.5 million. The numbers are probably greater than what is recorded and growing. Despite the bad press from national news broadcasts, homeschooling your children is one of the most unselfish acts you can do for your child. It's easy to send them off to public or private school and not have to concern yourself with the day to day grind of learning. Staying home full time and teaching your own children that takes patience and persistence and most of all: time. This long process takes practice to get the right learning style and curriculum so your child will receive an education.

As you start to think about homeschooling your child (and everyone does this) you have a mental picture of how you will teach or how your day will start and finish. You will think about all the wonderful learning experiences you will all have together in your classroom home and how wonderful your child will be. For the most part it is very rewarding to teach your own children but, there is an adjustment period that takes time until you are completely comfortable with what you are doing.

For most parents, the education they received themselves requires "unlearning" the way they learned. Homeschooling a child is not done the same way a public school teacher would teach a class of twenty students. Teaching one on one or one with two students is much more intimate and personal. It's almost like helping your child with his homework.

Next, if you hit schooling hard and heavy from the start, you will burn yourself out in a year. It is much more relaxed than people think. So what if your child doesn't finish all the textbooks and workbooks by the end of the "school year". So what if your child is not "up to grade" by the time he/she is seven years old. Public school grade levels were determined by other parents for someone else's child. Everyone has a different pace and you know your child better than anyone else.

Really what many parents would like their children to learn (besides being a good person) is how to think for themselves. From the book, *Home Built Discipline* by Raymond and Dorothy Moore talks about this very thing. They say that "learning to be thinkers rather than mere reflectors of others' thought should be the constant goal in the education of your children, both for their academic achievement and for character's sake". [6]

The Moores give us a simple recipe for making thinkers (remembering your close, affectionate, consistent attention to your children):

First, your truthful responsiveness is crucial. Meaning, don't give silly answers one time and serious answers another time. This does not mean you have no humor but being humorous for the sake of being funny is never appropriate if you want stable thinkers.

Second, remember not to expect much deep or consistent thoughtfulness of children under age eight and even less if they are younger.

Third, beginning at around ages three to five, ask why and how questions, first very simple ones and then more complex as they grow older. Don't demand deep or complex answers but be happy and especially attentive if your child has achieved this cognitive readiness earlier. If your child is a slow developer, don't feel disappointed with the answers.[7]

I think these are interesting ideas and have tried them out with my own children. Reading other homeschool advice helps me to find my own ground and be comfortable with my own ideas about how I should teach my children.

I am so happy to share this project with others who are curious about homeschooling or homeschoolers wanting more information. After reading through the other chapters, I have thought about the great diversity of the writings. I love the way the other mothers explained what they did and how they did it, writing in their own style. I hope you can appreciate the wealth of knowledge you have just read and can understand the life of homeschoolers. This chapter isn't the final word from all homeschoolers, just from me. There are many homeschool parents who write about what it is like and how to do it. If you are still curious or want more information, search those parents out. We love to talk about homeschooling to other interested people. Most importantly, educate your own children to be good people and to think for themselves.

Chapter 11
Homeschooling Resources

Collected by
Valerie J. Steimle

This last chapter is a resource guide for homeschoolers. One of the things I've learned over the years of homeschooling is the more you read, the more you learn. There is an incredible amount of information in books, homeschooling magazines and websites. It takes years to really get a good handle on all that information but this is a start. This is by far just a partial list. The more you dig, the more you will find. This is only the tip of the iceberg. Good luck.

Books: On homeschooling and children's intellectual, emotional and physical health. Most of these books can be found on Amazon.com

1. The Big Books of Home Learning—Mary Pride
   Volume I, II, III, IV   The basics of homeschooling from one of the pioneers of homeschooling.

2. School Proof-How to Help Your Family Beat the System and Learn to Love Learning The Easy, Natural Way by Mary Pride

3. The School in the Home by Thomas W. Evans

4. The Everything Homeschooling Book by Sherri Linsenback

5. The Successful Homeschool Family Handbook by Raymond and Dorothy Moore

6. Home Built Discipline by Raymond and Dorothy Moore

7. The Homeschooling Revolution by Isabel Lyman.

8. In Their Own Way by Thomas Armstrong, Ph.D.

9. The Myth of the A.D.D. Child - 50 Ways to Improve Your Child's Behavior and Attention Span Without Drugs, Labels, or Coercion by Thomas Armstrong, Ph.D.

10. Kinds of Smart: Identifying and Developing Your Multiple Intelligences by Thomas Armstrong, Ph.D.

11. The Einstein Syndrome by Thomas Sowell

12. Late-Talking Children by Thomas Sowell

13. Reclaiming Our Children: A Healing Solution for a Nation in Crisis by Peter R. Breggin, M.D.

14. Talking Back to Ritalin: What Doctors Aren't Telling You About Stimulants and ADHD by Peter R. Breggin, M.D.

Magazines: Online and otherwise:

1. Eclectic Homeschool Online: http://www.eho.org/ A complete homeschool magazine online for creative homeschoolers with feature articles, resources, reviews, a bookstore, advice column, and much more.

2. *F.U.N. News*: http://www.unschooling.org
Sample issue of the "Family Unschoolers Network" packed with lots of good features. Published quarterly, subscriptions and back issues available.

3. *Family Times*: www.homeeducator.com
From Home Educators. There are several articles available online.

4. *Growing Without Schooling*: www.holtgws.com
John Holt's magazine, *Growing Without Schooling*, is available for subscription. Online, find the table of contents of the current issue, read articles from early issues or order back issues in groups by topic.

5. *Home Education Learning Magazine*: http://educationalfreedom.com
HELM is a bimonthly print publication focusing on independent learning and self-directed education.

6. *Home Education Magazine*: http://www.home-ed-magazine.com/wlcm_HEM.html The oldest, most respected, and most informative homeschooling magazine.

7. *Homefires, the Journal of Homeschooling*: www.homefires.com
Home education resource guide for California and beyond.

8. *Homeschool Digest*: www.homeschooldigest.com
The quarterly journal for serious homeschoolers. The *Homeschool Digest* has a few articles from each issue online, subscribe by email or snail mail.

9. *Homeschooling Fun*: www.homschoolfun.com An online magazine for homeschool families. Lots of articles, a message board, lesson plans, and a discount bookstore.

10. *Homeschooling Today*: www.homschoolingtoday.com
A publication and an online source of ready-to-use curriculum, teaching tips, resources and encouragement for home educators.

11. *Homespun Solutions*:
http://members.aol.com/mwhomespun/welcome.htm
Newsletter for parents of children 3-8 committed to producing premium quality in-home learning experiences for families.

12. *Jewish Home Educator's Network*: http://snj.com/jhen
J.H.E.N. is a quarterly newsletter filled with a wide range of interesting topics, recipes, holiday and craft ideas, book reviews, a Jewish calendar, and help columns with practical how-to advice on homeschooling.

13. *Kid's Town*: www.hwcn.org/~ab448/kidstown
The magazine for homeschool kids by homeschool kids.

14. *Learners Online Magazine*:
www.learnersonline.com/magazine/magindex.htm
Learners Online helps teachers and home educators make the Net an accessible, useful educational tool. Each monthly issue gives you the knowledge and tools you need to integrate online content with traditional home and classroom learning.

15. *Natural Life*: www.life.ca/hs/index.html
Canadian publication that supports homeschooling and other ways of living naturally.

16. *Practical Homeschooling*: www.home-school.com
Published six times a year, *Practical Homeschooling* is available through subscription. The past issues are described on the site and can be ordered by telephone or mail.

17. *The Link*: www.homeschoolnewslink.com
A homeschool newspaper on the web with regular features by the Colfaxes and other leading homeschool writers.

18. *The Teaching Home*: www.teachinghome.com
A bimonthly magazine devoted to a Christian perspective of home education. Available by subscription.

Catalogues and Curriculums

1. Love to Learn, 1-888-771-1034- Working to make families stronger. Best educational resources.

2. Alpha Omega, 1-800-622-3070- Home Education Publication

3. CBD Home School, 1-800-247-4784- Educational Resources

4. Tobin's Lab, 1-800-522-4776- Hands on Science Materials for Families

5. Delta Education, 1-800-442-5444- Children learn by doing-Science and Math Resources

6. Lifetime Books and Gifts, (867) 676-6311-This catalogue is filled with so much homeschool information as well as curriculum information.

7. School of Tomorrow, (972) 315-1776 Accelerated Christian Education

8. Timberdoodle, (360) 426-0672- Many hands on and interesting books.

9. Calvert School, (410) 516-0337 - Curriculum through John Hopkins University.

10. Curriculum Associates Inc. 1-800-225-0248

11. Timberdoodle, 1-360-426-0672

12. Greenleaf Press, 1-615-449-1617

13. Elijah Company, 1-888-235-4524

14. Common Sense Press, 1-352-475-5757

15. Mind Ware, 1-800-999-0398

16. Key Curriculum Press, 1-800-995-MATH

17. Vertias Press, 1-800-922-5082

Websites:

1. Homeschool World: "The World's Most Visited Homeschool Site"
The latest homeschooling news, articles, organizations, events, Homeschool
Mall, and much, much more! K12 Lessons. ... Consult With a Homeschool
Expert! ...
http://www.home-school.com

2. Eclectic Homeschool Online - A Creative Homeschool Community
An online homeschool magazine and community with thousands of pages of
resources
and articles for creative, eclectic homeschoolers. ... Homeschool Extras. ...
http://www.eho.org

3. HSLDA | Home School Legal Defense Association: Homeschooling in ...
... the constitutional right of parents to direct the education of their children,
HSLDA is providing extensive on-line resources to the homeschool community.
...
http://www.hslda.org

4. American Homeschool Association
... Interviews with Homeschool Personalities. Information about Homeschooling
Resources. ... Websites
We Like. Information about the American Homeschool Association. ...
http://www.americanhomeschoolassociation.org

5. Free Homeschooling Resources from TheHomeSchoolMom.Com
... and more. Download our free homeschool planner. ...
TheHomeSchoolMom.Com,
Site Search, Bringing you the best free homeschool resources. ...
http://www.thehomeschoolmom.com/ -

6 Canadian home based learning
... Page. This site was formerly called the Canadian Homeschool Resource
Page. ... below. Canadian Homeschool Mail List: Living is learning. ...
http://www.flora.org/homeschool-ca

7. Canadian home based learning
... Page. This site was formerly called the Canadian Homeschool Resource
Page. Canadian Homeschool Mail List: Living is learning.
http://www.flora.org/homeschool-ca

8. Laurel Springs Homeschool
Accredited, K-12, Online/Text & Teachers, Learning Styles Profiles
www.laurelsprings.com

9. Welcome - Jon's Homeschool Resources
Jon's Homeschool Resources is perhaps the oldest and largest collection of
homeschool
resources on the Web - online support groups, offline support groups for ...
http://www.midnightbeach.com/hs

10. Homeschool Search Engine
Homeschool Search Engine.
http://www.homeschool.sites.cc/

11. Homeschooling Zone Main Page
Homeschool Zone is a community of homeschoolers, afterschoolers,
parents, and educators. FREE newsletters; support groups. ...
http://www.homeschoolzone.com/main.htm

12. Homeschool Social Register
Get in touch with other homeschoolers and unschoolers in your area. Build your
own custom page of homeschool resources. ... The Homeschool Social Register.
...
http://www.homeschoolmedia.net/register/index.phtml

13. Homeschool Math - free worksheets and homeschooling resources
Homeschool Math is a comprehensive math resource site for homeschooling
parents
and teachers: find a homeschool math curriculum guide, free worksheets, math
...
http://www.homeschoolmath.net/

14. Homeschool Associates: Serving the nation's home school community ...
... Get a real High School Diploma for your homeschool work. ... Stop paying too
much

for your homeschool books and start saving at the Bookmobile Online. ...
http://www.homeschoolassociates.com/

15. Home Schooling Curriculum for Math, English Grammar, History ...
(800)401-9931
http://www.homeschooldiscount.com/

16. Home Sweet Home School - Resources, Links & Information
Hundreds of eclectic homeschool links on curriculum, resources, virtual field trips,
and more, as well as forums that include articles and a message board on ...
http://home-educate.com

17. Pagan Homeschool Page
The Pagan Homeschool Page offers a variety of fun activities, homeschooling information,
and networking opportunities for Pagan homeschooling families. ...
http://www.homestead.com/barbooch/PaganHomeschool.html

18. The Homeschool Connexion
The Homeschool Connexion: An online community completely for and by homeschooled
youth featuring a web-zine with new articles published weekly, a forum.
http://www.hsconnexion.com/

19. Crosswalk.com - home_school
Search Crosswalk Search: In: home school. Newsletters. Crosswalk Home School
Update. Crosswalk Home School News. Crosswalk Home School Life. ...
http://homeschool.crosswalk.com/

20. About Homeschooling - Homeschooling Information and Homeschool ...
THE starting place for exploring homeschooling. Find everything from how to get
started in homeschooling to homeschool resources for the more experienced. ...
http://homeschooling.about.com/

About the Author

Valerie J. Steimle has been homeschooling her children since 1990. She has been researching and writing about family issues since that time and has had numerous articles published. She has been involved in many community organizations from education to the Save-a-Life foundation. She graduated from Ricks College in Rexburg Idaho in 1977 and then attended Brigham Young University in Provo, Utah in special education.

She is the mother of nine children and will soon become a grandmother. She has just recently become widowed and has put all her efforts into raising the rest of her children at home and writing in defense of the family. See www.goodmorningplanetearth.com. She is also the author of **Home Is Where The Heart Is.**

Endnotes

[1] LeAnne Weiss, *Heartlifters for Mom,* Howard Publishing, West Monroe, Louisiana, 2000, pages 1-3.

[2] *The Elijah Company* Catalogue, Crossville, TN. 2002, page 5.

[3] Dr. Raymond Moore, Dorothy Moore, *The Successful Homeschool Family Handbook*, Thomas Nelson Inc, Nashville, TN, 1994, pages

[4] See www.hslda.org

[5] www.WorldNetDaily.com,posted October 23, 2003 called: "Homeschoolers New Political Force Refutes 'Socialization' Concerns Posed By Thinkers In Academia",

[6] Raymond and Dorothy Moore, *Home Built Discipline*, Thomas Nelson Publishers, Nashville, Tennessee, 1987, page 139.

[7] Ibid.

All quotations used in this book came from one of the following internet resources under the subject on education:

1. www.brainyquote.com
2. www.quotationspage.com
3. www.quoteland.com
4. www.aphids.com/quotes/index.shtml.
5. www.goodquotes.com